Date Due		
MAY 1 2 1992		
MAY 2 2 1992		
NOV 2 9 1993		
MAR 1 0 1997		
JUN 0 2 1998		
NOV 1 0 1999		
OCT 0 7 2003		
SEP 2 3 2004		

Books by KURT E. KOCH

Between Christ & Satan
Christian Counseling and Occultism
Coming One
Day X
Demonology, Past and Present
Devil's Alphabet
Occult Bondage and Deliverance
Revival Fires in Canada
Revival in Indonesia
Victory Through Persecution
World Without Chance?

DEMONOLOGY,

PAST AND PRESENT

Kurt E. Koch, Th.D.

KREGEL PUBLICATIONS
Grand Rapids, Michigan 49501

Library of Congress Catalog Card Number 72-93353
ISBN 0-8254-3013-5

First American Edition 1973
Reprinted 1978

PRINTED IN THE UNITED STATES OF AMERICA

— CONTENTS —

Preface   **Page**

1. Christian Counseling and Occultism. 9

2. Demonology, Past and Present. 21

3. Mediumistic Powers, Natural Powers and Spiritual Gifts. 53

4. Occult Subjection, the Neglect Factor in Mental Illnesses 75

5. Miracles of Healing Today — Their Biblical, Suggestive or Demonic Character 104

6. Demon Possession and Deliverance 131

PREFACE

It was Dr. Fred Dickason of the Moody Bible Institute who first put the idea of this book into my mind. He had invited me to speak at the Moody Theological Lectureship in Chicago. After the meeting, a number of students asked me if they could have a copy of my message, and I willingly agreed to let them duplicate the address. It was this, together with the many similar requests that I have had all over the world, which finally persuaded me that a book comprising of a set of addresses I have given on occultism would be a worthwhile project.

I would therefore ask the reader to remember that each chapter of this book is basically a unit in itself, and that they were not originally designed to follow one another as the chapters in a normal book. Inevitably some of the ground will be covered more than once, since the basic facts concerning demonology are the same whether one is in Japan, Buenos Aires or anywhere else in the world. In spite of the repetition, however, the emphasis of the various addresses is never the same. Moreover, the examples I have chosen to illustrate the talks are different in each case.

There is an increasing chaos growing in the intellectual and spiritual climate of our day. This is evidenced in many ways, a few of which I will quickly mention:

1. In the natural sciences the importance of reason is becoming overemphasized. *Ratio mensura omnium rerem* — ratio is the measure of all.

2. An unquenchable thirst in the soul of man is promoting an increase in all forms of mysticism, spiritism and musical ecstasy.
3. Mankind's sensual desires are promoting an increase in sexual, alcoholic, and drug licentiousness.
4. An overemphasis of the irrational is producing a growth in magic and other mediumistic practices.
5. The heightening of the spiritual need of our times has led to the birth of the so-called charismatic movement and other extreme religious tendencies.
6. The 'pandemonium' of our times is most terribly evident in the Judas, Spiritistic and Satan Cults which have recently sprung up in different parts of the world. Anston LaVey, the self-appointed devil's pope from San Francisco, claims to have some 200,000 followers throughout the world, all of whom have subscribed themselves to the devil with their own blood.

In order to face this chaos which is developing in the world as the Second Coming of Christ draws nearer, Christians are in need of three things: a firm grounding in the Word of God; a fresh infilling of the Holy Spirit; the gift of the discernment of spirits. It is only in this way that we can hope to avoid being destroyed in this witch's cauldron. Probably what we should desire more than anything else is an all-embracing revival in which all the gifts and powers of the Holy Spirit are seen to be present and alive in the Church once more. But God is sovereign and we cannot force him to act. It remains for us to do but one thing — to pray!

Kurt E. Koch

Chapter 1

CHRISTIAN COUNSELING AND OCCULTISM

(An Address given at a Ministers' meeting in Cape Town, South Africa)

Summary

Neurosis And Occult Practices
  I. Different Forms of Superstition
 II. Fortune-telling and its Effects
III. Magic and the Danger it Involves
IV. Spiritism and its Damage to Spiritual Life
 V. Deliverance from Occult Bondage

CHRISTIAN COUNSELING AND OCCULTISM

My work among the emotionally and psychically disturbed stretches back now to something in the region of forty years. During this time I have personally counselled some 20,000 different people. All this has made it clear to me that in cases of depression, between 5% and 10% of sufferers have either had contact with occultism themselves or have ancestors who have dabbled in the same, and in cases of mental illness the percentage is much higher; in Germany and Switzerland 25% to 35%, and in England and California between 40% and 50%. On the island of Bali, local doctors estimate that the percentage is even higher and they report that about 85% of those suffering from psychiatric illnesses come from families in which occultism is practiced.

In all this, however, we must be careful not to deduce a simple law of cause and effect. Many depressed and neurotic people have had no contact with occultism at all, while many others only become involved in spiritism etc. after they have become emotionally or mentally disturbed. One can only apply the term occult subjection or bondage to those people whose mental or emotional problems stem from the practice of magic or sorcery. The word 'occult' comes from the Latin word 'occultus' which means: hidden, secret, sinister, dark or mysterious. The term can be applied in general to extra-sensory experiences and phenomena which parapsychology makes the subject of its study. But it is not here that my main interest lies. I am rather concerned in the counselling aspect and I would prefer to define my ministry as that of informing, warning and giving aid.

Occultism can be summarized under four different headings.

I. *Superstition.*

Here are a few examples: In Japan the number four is feared and avoided by many people. Some hotels refuse to use the number. In the same way some Japanese will refuse to accept a telephone number if it contains several fours in it. Why is this? The word four in Japanese is 'shi'. and 'shi' is also the word for death. Hence people not wanting to be associated with death avoid the number four. In Europe the number thirteen has the same effect. When I was a student, the room I was in was numbered 12a. When I asked the bursar if he would change the number back to 13 — I told him I was not superstitious — he agreed to have it altered. However, when the painter arrived, he refused to change the number because he maintained that he did not want to be responsible for making the room unlucky. Thousands of these unreasonable superstitious ideas exist all over the world. To see a spider in the morning ruins some people's day; if a black cat walks across the path of a hunter he must return home straight away; to hear the cry of a barn owl is meant to herald death; a four leaf clover or to see a chimney sweep is supposed to bring a person luck; so we could go on.

The Scriptures declare that we are not to give

ear to signs and omens. Only those who abandon their faith fall prey to superstition and unbelief and succumb to the influence of ungodly powers.

II. *Fortune-telling.*

There are many types of fortune telling abroad. Horoscopes, palmistry, the use of a rod and pendulum, card laying, reading tea-leaves are the names of but a few. Some fortune-tellers use a crystal ball, others fall into a trance, but perhaps the most dangerous type are those who hide behind a religious facade. Acts 16 refers to a case in point. The girl with the spirit of divination at Phillippi followed Paul and his companions, shouting: "These men are servants of the Most High God." This was, of course, true. But Paul turned to her and said, "I command you in the Name of Jesus to come out of her." The young girl was delivered.

People with the gift of discernment like Paul are hard to find today. Many Christians, for example, consider Jean Dixon to be a prophetess simply because she attends the Catholic mass and prays the 23rd Psalm, yet if Paul were alive today, he would simply say to her, "Depart from me, you have an unclean spirit." Jean Dixon, far from being a prophetess, is a dangerous fortune-teller with a spirit of divination.

What I am saying here is not just based upon the opinion of one man, I can actually cite emotional disturbances which have arisen as a direct result of her fortune telling. An American woman confessed to me that after she had visited Jean Dixon she had entirely lost her desire to pray. Whenever she had tried to read the Bible her vision had become blurred, and at night she had been haunted by apparitions. None of this had occurred until after the meeting with Jean Dixon.

France, too, has its own dangerous fortune teller. One of his methods is to study his visitor's eyes, a common practice among occultists. Let us quickly add though, that such a practice can have a legitimate basis too. This Frenchman, however, on looking into the eyes of a young woman, told her, "You are going to have five children, but you will die after the birth of the fifth child." No, this was not a legitimate form of eye-diagnosis, it was a case of pure fortune-telling. Later when the fifth child was born, there was much concern in the family. Finally the grandmother came to me privately and said, "My daughter is going to die." I was angry that such a delusion and lack of faith could exist. How can a fortune teller or an eye-diagnostician know when a person is going to die? This is God's domain. Suffice it to say, however, that neither the child nor the mother suffered any ill effects. The Frenchman, far from being a specialist, was merely a liar and a fraud whose practice ought to be stopped. Such people are specialists only at causing neuroses in their clients. And this also applies to those newspaper editors who allow horoscopes to be printed in their publications. As it was said a long time ago, they do not know what they are doing. It is only the counsellor who realizes the effects as he deals with those who come to him for help.

III. *Magic.*

This form of occultism appears under many guises. There is the magical infliction of disease, magical healing, love and hate magic, magic persecution, defense magic, and worst of all, death magic.

Magical healing is the commonest form one meets today. There are many magical healers, fetish healers, psychometric healers, spiritistic healers, magnetopathic healers and so on. I will only be able to make a few comments on the problem, but if you want a more detailed account of the factors involved I would refer you to my English and German books.

Many strange practices are connected with healing magic. Christian Science healers make a technical use of Bible verses in conjunction with autosuggestion. This is a clear misuse of the words of Scripture. Fetish healers accomplish their work by means of fetishes or amulets. In Indonesia, people are given stones which have been dedicated to Satan. In the religious world, similar practices are common. Relics, holy water, consecrated oil, blessed handkerchiefs or small pictures of the saints are given to the 'faithful' to heal them from disease. Psychometric healers ask their patients to give them an object which they then use as a contact-bridge. It might be some hair, a piece of a fingernail, some article of clothing, or even some saliva on a piece of paper. These are used by the healer to diagnose the disease and to produce the healing influence on the patient. Is this really possible, one is forced to ask? Besides the great deal of deception and fraud practiced, there is a form of healing and a form of health to be obtained from genuine healers. But the cost is great. The spiritual life of the person healed is put into bondage, imprisoned, or even killed. Occult healings really do exist, even demonic healings can be substantiated, but the result is a bondage of the soul to the forces of the devil. When Satan heals a person of tuberculosis of the lungs or of cancer, he afterwards presents his bill: the eternal life of the soul.[1]

Magic has been used in all departments of life. I will quote just one example of love magic. I was told the story when visiting the Solomon Islands. A girl had wanted to get married, but since she was so ugly none of the men wanted to marry her. She visited a magician and he gave her some herbs which she mixed in the food of the man she loved. The young man came under the power of the spell and found himself compelled in an inexplicable way to marry the girl. The love potion was a success!

IV. *Spiritism.*

Leaving behind the realms of magic, we come now to the area of ancestor-worship and spirit and demon cults. Spiritism occurs in many forms: table-lifting, glass-moving, the use of the ouija-board, automatic writing, trances, materialization, astral travelling, psychokinesis, apports, levitation and more.

Among Christians there are many who suffer from a strange blindness to the dangers of these practices. Many in fact hold that things like glass-

---

[1]See Chapter 5.

moving and the ouija-board are harmless party games. On the other hand, rationalists write all these phenomena off as make-believe or fraud. If this were really so, however, why is it that the Bible so clearly warns us against practicing them? The Old Testament declares that anyone who does these things is an abomination to the Lord. King Saul was actually destroyed following his resorting to a medium for help. I know of pastors, and even missionaries and evangelists who have been similarly destroyed by spiritism. People who have grown up in a family in which spiritism is practised find themselves burdened by it. They find belief an impossibility. They find they cannot accept Jesus as Lord, and they cannot pray - unless the Lord Himself steps in and delivers them from the ban.

In England, I met an Anglican minister who had, on one occasion, taken part in some table-lifting. Afterwards he found that his spiritual life became, as it were, dammed up; he began to entertain strange and erroneous teachings in his mind, and at a meeting at which I spoke he attacked me publicly. Later, however, he could go on no longer, and he called on me to ask for my help. The Lord worked a great miracle in his life and set him free. Afterwards, instead of opposing my message, he asked me to take a series of meetings at his Church.

I find myself duty-bound to warn people as strongly as I can against spiritism. Our psychiatrists are inundated by people who have inherited the effects of spiritism from their ancestors. But there is seldom any help to be found. The reason is clear, for the complaint is not organically or psychically based but is rather spiritual. The root is occult.

V. *Deliverance.*

To finish my talk without mentioning deliverance would be worse than having never spoken at all. So I say clearly: deliverance and help are at hand. A person has come into this world whose power exceeds all that of the devil and hell. His Name is Jesus. As the New Testament declares: "For this purpose the Son of God was manifested, that He might destroy the works of the devil." Satan cannot stand in the presence of the Son of God.

Let me give an illustration of this. I once spoke at a Bible School in Singapore. Afterwards, one of the students rose to her feet and gave her testimony. She had not been a Christian for very long when one of her friends had asked her to join in a game involving a ouija-board. The girl did not know what the game was and so she went along. When the group had started asking the board questions nothing happened. The small glass only trembled but did not move. Finally, the spokesman for the group asked, "Is something disturbing you?" "Yes," came the immediate reply. By now the young Christian had begun to feel uneasy, and so she left the room. The three remaining continued with their game. "What has disturbed you?" they went on. "The girl who has just left the room," came the reply. "But why did she worry you?" they asked. "Because, with her -

is God!" The position here is clear. The satanic spirit whose power was behind the ouija-board was unable to stand before the faith of the young born-again girl.

American psychologists have maintained that the force which makes the glass move is drawn from the subconscious minds of the people. This, however, can be easily refuted. Through the ouija-board and glass-moving, events are predicted and statements made which can in no wise be attributed to the subconscious. And on top of this, the power at work is overcome through the prayers of a Christian. This could be illustrated time and time again. Therefore, whatever reasons you may try to give, never become involved in experiments in this field. If you play with fire you will get your fingers burnt! We must hold on to the One who has received all power both in heaven and on earth. Yes, Jesus Christ has crushed the serpent's head, and his followers have the right to follow in their victor's train.

Chapter 2

DEMONOLOGY, PAST AND PRESENT

(An address given at the 4th Annual Theological Lectureship at Moody Bible Institute on October 15th, 1971).

Summary

    I The Definition of the Demonic.
   II Demonism and Animism.
  III Demonism and Hellenism.
  IV Demonism in the Old Testament.
   V Demonism in the New Testament.
  VI Demonism in Church History.
 VII Demonism in the Present Century.
      A.   On the Theological Front
      B.   On the Psychiatric Front.
      C.   On the Psychical Front.
      D.   In Christian Counselling.
VIII The Christian's Position.

DEMONOLOGY, PAST AND PRESENT

I.   Before we begin to talk about demons, we must first explain the meaning of the word. This is not as easy as it may seem. An example will help illustrate what I mean.

During my missionary travels, I have on several occasions come across the terrible custom of eating the dead. The custom is most pronounced among the Pacaas Novos, a tribe of Indians living on the border between Brazil and Bolivia. Their existence was only discovered some ten years ago. There are two types of corpse eating: a ritual form and a common form. The chief, the witch doctor and the elders of the tribe participate in the ritual form. The relatives and the kinsmen of the deceased take part in the common or familiar form.

The meaning of the word 'demon' can be traced back to this custom which has been practiced among the heathen for thousands of years. The word 'demon' contains the Greek root 'dia' or 'daiomai', meaning 'to divide, to tear or to portion out'. People who ate their dead were therefore called 'demons' or 'dividers'. One can find this derivation of the word in the large Kittel's Greek dictionary.

Another facet of heathenism throws even greater light on the origin of the word. The cannibals of New Guinea actually call the souls of the dead 'demons'.

It is worth noting therefore, for those interested in the growth and development of religious ideas, that the demonic is connected with eating the dead and cannibalism both among primitive tribes in both South America and East Africa.

We must look more closely at the term now and see what further ideas underlie the word 'demonic'.

II.   *Demonism and Animism.*

In the Greek language, the word 'demon' has strong connections with the idea of animism. Animism comes from the word 'anima' meaning 'soul' or 'life', and is the doctrine that objects in nature possess, or are possessed, by souls or spirits, and it embraces the idea of pantheism as well. These souls and spirits are those of the dead, and they are regarded as immaterial and intermediary beings. Such animistic concepts, together with spiritism, still form the basis of the ancestor-worship found in East Asia today. The Japanese continue to pray to the spirits of their ancestors and to offer sacrifices of food to them, while spiritistic cults contact and address the spirits of the dead.

The animist believes that these spirits are either good or evil in character and sacrifices are made to placate those they regard as bad. In spiritistic circles, too, this belief in good and evil spirits persists. This has given rise to the various forms of spiritism ranging from the criminal macumba and voodoo cults, to the social and religious spiritistic movements, as, for example, the Umbanda and Kardec groups in Brazil.

III. *Demonism and Hellenism.*

The influence of animistic ideas about demonology can be traced in Greek philosophy. The popular belief that immaterial beings could act as protecting spirits was gradually accepted by the Greeks. As time passed, the efficacy and various tasks of these spirits was gradually more clearly defined, with the result that a heirarchy of demons, arranged in various classes, came into being. At the same time, the evil nature of the demons became more and more pronounced, and we find that Empedokles and Plato, and later Plutarch all blamed the demons not only for possession, but for disease and natural catastrophes as well. Finally, among the Stoics, the idea developed that the demons, magic and mantic, were all inseparably linked.

A belief in ghosts was also associated with the spirits of the dead. Pliny, in the middle of the second century, described a haunted house in Athens where a white figure used to appear each night. Later excavation revealed that there was a skeleton buried at the exact place where the ghost used to appear. After it was removed and buried in a proper fashion, the haunting ceased.

There are many parallels, even today, to this ancient story concerning apparitions of the dead.

IV. *Demonism in the Old Testament.*

We now turn to the question of demonism

as we find it mentioned in the Old Testament. But first of all, I must make it clear from what standpoint we are approaching the problem. If one fails to start from the correct point, one will never find the key to understanding the Old Testament. It was Archimedes who said, "Dos moi po sten kei kina ten gan" — Give me a fixed point and I will move the earth.

There are two ways of approaching the Old Testament.

A. As a student I was able to listen to Martin Dibelius, who, as a well-known member of the school of form critics, looked upon the Old and New Testaments as merely the reflection of ancient mythology. This theological school of thought maintains that the Bible is founded upon oriental folklore and myth. One can only hope to reach the core of truth within it through a process of demythologising. Even as a student, however, I was unable to accept this idea, and I soon came to the conclusion that it was the theologians who needed demythologising and not the Bible!

B. The second method of approach is to accept the Bible as what it claims to be: the inspired Word of God. In 2 Peter 1:21 we read: "No prophecy ever came by the impulse of man, but men moved by the Holy Spirit spoke from God." Similarly in 2 Timothy 3:16 Paul writes: "Pasa graphe theopneustos" — all Scripture is inspired of God. It was on this foundation that Luther stood when he declared: "The Holy Scriptures are our sole authority in matters of faith and conduct."

The problem facing us is fundamental: what, or who, is our authority? Do we assess the Bible using myths as our guide or do we use the Bible to judge the myths? What is our position? Paul wrote in 1 Corinthians 2:14: "The natural man does not receive the things of the Spirit of God, but the spiritual man judges and understands all things."

This gives us the fixed point we have been looking for. The Scriptures, inspired as they are by the Holy Spirit, are the pivot for which we seek.

It is absolutely essential that we clarify our position, particularly when we are dealing with the demonic, since theologians are inclined to make the most absurd assertions when dogmatising about this subject.

In the Old Testament we find a clear distinction drawn between the angels of God (Psalm 91, Daniel 9:21) and the fallen angels (Genesis 5), both of which are understood to be immaterial beings. The new idea which comes out however, is that there is no connection at all between good and evil spirits. Unlike in animism and Greek philosophy, the demons are unable to play a double role. Moreover the so-called spirits of the dead play only a very minor part in the Old Testament story.

They are mentioned in 1 Samuel 28 and in Isaiah 8:19, but elsewhere communication with the dead is bracketed together with sorcery, and forbidden under the threat of death. (Deuteronomy 18:10-18).

I am sometimes asked when talking about this subject, whether or not the old man who appeared to Saul at Endor was really Samuel. The answer is not all that easy. Luther maintained that it could hardly have been Samuel since this would contradict the rest of Scripture. On the other hand Jacob Spenyer, one of the fathers of Pietism, maintained that it was Samuel. Can one say which is right?

To try and understand the story one must approach it from both the Biblical and the counselling point of view. In the story of Balaam and Balak, Balak wanted Balaam to bring a curse on Israel. Although Balaam at heart had no qualms about this, God forbade him from doing so and made him bless Israel instead. When Balak rebuked him, he could only reply: "I cannot resist God." This gives us a clue as to what took place at Endor. When spiritistic mediums call upon the dead the seance is usually conducted calmly and without fuss. In 1 Samuel 28 however, something dramatic took place which made the woman acting as medium cry out in terror, "Why have you deceived me? You are Saul." An examination of the text reveals an excitement which does not normally exist in a spiritistic meeting. What had happened? The answer is that God had taken the matter out of the woman's hands, just as he had done so with Balaam, and he had sent the real Samuel thereby bypassing the incantations of the woman. In this way Saul heard his own death sentence from the mouth of Samuel himself.

V. *Demonism in the New Testament.*

The New Testament leads us still further in our understanding of this problem. First of all though, I will mention a few philological facts. The noun 'demon' only occurs once in the New Testament, in Matthew 8:31. The adjective 'demonic' on the other hand occurs more than 50 times in the Gospels. Evil or unclean spirits are mentioned 28 times, but there is no mention of the spirits of the dead. The angels of God (Matthew 25:31, Luke 12:8, 15:10, John 1:51) and the angels of Satan (Matthew 25:41, 2 Corinthians 12:7, Revelation 12:7) are still sharply contrasted as in the Old Testament, and contact with the powers of Satan through participation in heathen rites and sorcery (1 Corinthians 10:20) equally warned against (Galatians 5:20, Revelation 9:21, 18:23, 22:15).

The New Testament goes on to describe the war which exists between the 'civitas Dei' and the 'civitas diaboli' — the kingdom of God and the kingdom of Satan — a struggle in which man is also involved. Ephesians 6:12 describes how "we are not contending against flesh and blood, but against the spiritual hosts of wickedness in the heavenly places", and in 1 Peter 5:8 we find the words, "Your adversary the devil prowls around like a roaring lion, seeking whom he may devour." Yet thanks be to God that "He gives us the victory through Jesus Christ our Lord." (1 Corinthians 15:57).

This introduces us to an entirely new concept with regard to the question of the demonic. Jesus entered human history and thereby made an end to all the powers of the devil. Colossians 2:15 reads: "Christ disarmed the principalities and powers — dunamais, thronoi, exousiai, kuriotetes, archei — and made a public example of them, triumphing over them in his cross."

With the coming of the Lord, the age of myths was over. As Peter testified (2 Peter 1:16): "We have not followed cleverly devised myths . . . but were eyewitnesses of his majesty."

Yes, with the coming of the Lord, the power of the demons was finished. Whenever Jesus came face to face with the ranks of the enemy they were forced to leave the field (Mark 5, Luke 8). At His word the power of the demons was defeated.

VI.   *Demonism in Church History.*

The problem of the demonic has always been an acute one throughout the history of the Church. It is sad, but true, to say that whenever the Church of Christ has failed to give the Holy Spirit his rightful place, the powers of darkness have always filled the gap. The medieval cults of Satan and the black masses are but evidence of this fact.

Another indication of the depths to which the Church has fallen is seen in the Papal Bull 'Vox in Rama' in 1233 and that of Innocent VIII in 1484. The infamous 'Witches' Hammer' (Malleus Malifacarum) as conceived by the Dominican monks, bears similar testimony to the terrible attitude which existed at that time towards the demonic. This latter document alone was responsible for the deaths of thousands of innocent people, and it was not until 1869 that the last so-called heretic of the inquisition was burnt at the stake in Madrid.

More recently, as the age of enlightenment dawned, belief in the demonic has declined among people in the West, although it did not disappear altogether.

VII. *Demonism in the Present Century.*

Over the last few decades the question of the demonic has again raised its head, and in some quarters the problem has become acute.

A.   On the theological front liberal and neo-rationalistic theologians continue to deny the existence of not only Satan, but of the angels and demons as well. As they see it the demonic is merely the reflection of either the sub- or super-conscious within man. It is therefore, rather an imminent problem than a transcendental or metaphysical one.

To such people the stories in the New Testament concerning those who were demon possessed, simply mean that Jesus was a child of his own times, holding the primitive concepts of those around him. Possession is therefore, a form of mental illness — at least, this is what they say.

The New Testament itself points out the error of such an outlook. The Gospels clearly differentiate between possession and pathological disturbances (Matthew 4:24, Mark 1:32, Matthew 8:16).

Reports of possession are uncomfortable for our modern liberal scholars. They do not quite fit into their rationalistic scheme of the world. Bultmann, for example, could do no more than describe the story of the possessed Gadarene as a 'terrible account'.

B. There is also conflict concerning the demonic on the psychiatric front.

1. I was once invited by Dr. Martin Lloyd-Jones to speak before a group of psychiatrists in London. During the discussion which followed my talk, two psychiatrists stood up and stated quite dogmatically that possession as such did not exist. Immediately after this, however, two other psychiatrists present — they were both Christians — rose to their feet and said that they were not only convinced that possession was a genuine phenomenon, but that they had already come across cases of it within their own practice, one of them seven cases and the other eleven.

2. In general, within the psychiatric world anyone who talks as if demons really exist is looked upon as being rather old-fashioned or backward in his thinking. One psychiatrist in Germany, in spite of claiming to be a Christian, published an essay in which he maintained that the possessed Gadarene was merely suffering from a severe case of hysteria. The reason the man lived among the tombs, he said, was to draw attention to himself. He had only come to Jesus in order to be associated with the famous healer he had heard about. By becoming one of his disciples he thought that he would become famous too. This effort on behalf of a so-called Christian psychiatrist to explain away the supernatural by means of the natural is typical of the attitude today. The apostle Paul is quite clear concerning such speculation: "Claiming to be wise, they have become fools."

3. About the most interesting discussion I have had with a group of psychiatrists was at the University of Freiburg. I had been invited to speak on the subject of possession. Even before I arrived I knew that there was sure to be a good deal of heated discussion after my talk, but I willingly accepted the invitation. As it happened, after I had finished speaking, the Superintendent of the University clinic introduced a patient to us, named Maria. She had been

sent to them by a Roman Catholic Bishop who had described her as being possessed. The professor remarked with some annoyance in his tone, "How can a Bishop be so old-fashioned as to still believe in demon possession in the twentieth century?"

The patient's symptoms were described to us, and the audience, consisting as it did of doctors, psychologists, psychiatrists and a few theologians, was asked for its opinions. Let me briefly describe some of what was said.

It was maintained that Maria would somtimes cry out and scream, "I'm being strangled by a snake." Although no snake was ever present, the marks of the 'coils' were clearly visible on her skin. At other times she would suddenly change her voice and men's voices would speak out of her. The professor told us that on being questioned the voices had replied, "We are seven devils." She would also act as if she was being struck by an invisible force, and the weals which had appeared on her body at such times had actually been photographed. Strangest of all, Maria had the ability to predict the future. She was, in fact, clairvoyant.

"What do you make of all this?" the professor asked, turning to some Catholic theologians present. Their reply was quite definite and immediate, "It's clearly a case of possession." "But you can't say that," responded the professor angrily, "There's

no such thing as possession!" Then he
addressed me with the same question.
"Before I answer," I replied, "could you
tell me whether Maria ever dabbled in
magic or spiritism before her illness
began?" "Why yes," he answered, "it is
recorded in her case history. But that has
nothing to do with my question." "Oh yes
it has," I went on. "Over the past 40 years
I have met with numerous examples just as
you have described, and I would say that
beyond any doubt Maria is demon possessed."

The professor, a psychiatrist, but not
a Christian, could not agree with me. The
only thing he was prepared to do was to
admit that he had never before met a case
as puzzling as Maria's.

C. The influence of the demonic can be seen
    on the psychical front. A whole host of
    questions present themselves to us in this
    realm. Why, for example, has there been
    such a growth in recent years of sexual
    laxity, drug addiction, racism, world com-
    munism, occultism, spiritism, and theologi-
    cal extremism? Why has so much chaos and
    despair followed in its wake? We have only
    time to touch on a few of the answers.

1. Firstly, due to the higher living standards
    for which the West has now become re-
    nowned, the over-saturated population is
    being forced continually to seek satisfac-

tion from new stimulants for its insatiable passions and desires.

2. Secondly, in the West people are becoming perplexed and insecure. The world is becoming barren of new intellectual ideas, of lasting ideals, and of men to lead it out of the desert in which it finds itself. The resultant insecurity leads directly to the instability and escapism and intellectual substitutes surrounding us today.

3. Then again, increased technological advance has left a spiritual vacuum into which innumerable psychic forces have flooded. One would be surprised if one knew just how many of our so-called scientists and intellectuals are turning to spiritism in order to find some sort of spiritual relief.

4. But there are other reasons which are weightier still. The present generation is sick and bleeds from a thousand wounds. At our psychiatric conferences, more and more distressing facts are coming to light. In Switzerland, for example, 4% of all hospital beds are for the mentally depressed. In Germany the percentage is 10%, in England 25%, while in America it has reached the devastating level of 50%. The world is becoming more neurotic every day!

5. The statements of many of our leaders are also very disquieting. We are living in a

climate very similar to that of ancient Rome. Civilization seems to be marching towards its own destruction, as books like Gordon R. Taylor's Doomsday book describes. At most, the world's natural resources can only last another 100 years.

6. The clearest answer to the chaotic conditions of our times is found in the Bible. We are living in the Last Days. The final pages of history are now being read. We see this through passages like 1 Timothy 4:1 and 2 Timothy 3:1-4. This century can only be understood aright in the light of the prophetic word. Satan is mobilizing all his forces for an all-out attack. The demonic world has entered the final lap. It is these facts that enable us to understand fully the extremism which is appearing on every side. To fail therefore, to take our stand at the foot of the cross, to fail to build our house upon the Rock, is to be swept away by the turmoil of the End-time. We are living in days of a demonic nature!

Perhaps an example can help explain what I mean. A few years ago I was conselling a possessed theological student. As I was praying for him, he suddenly fell into a trance and we heard strange voices speaking out of him in foreign languages. "Who are you?" I asked the voices. They replied in English, "We are 50 demons." I went on, "In the Name of Jesus Christ I command you to come out of him." "Don't mention

that name," the voices screamed, "we cannot bear it." During the battle which followed, the demonic voices cried out, "The
Lord is coming soon with his holy angels.
Give us more time. We will be finished
when he comes."[1]

Do not misunderstand me. We do not
need the testimony of demons to know
that Jesus is coming soon. It is interesting,
however, to note that what modern theologians deny, the demons testify took in fear.

D. Another area in which the demonic is
making itself known is that of Christian
counselling.

For almost forty years now I have
been counselling people who have suffered
as a result of occultism, and in the thousands
of cases I have dealt with I have made two
significant discoveries.

1. Demonically oppressed people exhibit the
same symptoms today as did the possessed
Gadarene almost two thousand years ago.
Demon possession has therefore remained
the same in its effects since the time of
Christ, despite what the modernists would
try to say to the contrary.

2. The second discovery I have made is that
possession as well as not altering with time,
does not alter with place either. A possessed person in Haiti behaves in the same

---

[1] For further details see Chapter 5.

way as a possessed person in New Guinea. There are, therefore, these two constants connected with demon possession: the first is that neither time, age nor epoch affects the phenomenon, and the second is that neither geographical, national, racial nor cultural factors affect its outworking.

The question facing us is therefore, what conclusions are we to draw from these two observations? A psychologist might be tempted to write the matter off by referring to the principle of archetypes. Yet this term, as formulated by Professor C. G. Jung fails to do justice to the phenomenon. Possession in all its different facets fails to fit into the normal psychological and psychiatric pattern. Let it also be noted if in passing that although the theories of psychiatry and psychology change from decade to decade, the fact of possession remains unchanged. These two branches of science are in fact indifferent to religious values, unlike the possessed person who reacts strongly whenever he is faced with genuine spiritual counsel. This reaction, called the phenomenon of resistance, is illustrated in the following example.

I knew of one possessed woman who could not even look at a Bible or crucifix during the occasions of her attacks. It is true that anti-religious complexes are known to exist in the medical world — these often result from an atheistic or an over-religious upbringing — but in cases of posesssion, the phenomenon of resistance is so clearly defined that it is insufficient to merely label it as just a complex.

For example, in Berne in Switzerland, I once had to counsel another woman with the marked characteristics of possession. She told me that whenever she entered a Christian home she always began to feel sick. In the same way, if she was travelling through an unfamiliar town after dark, she would always begin to feel sick on passing a church, even if at first unaware of its presence. A feeling of loathing would also come over her if a Christian got on the same tram, and she did not have to recognize the person for this to take place. She went on to describe that because of this she could tell the difference between nominal and genuine Christians, and this was particularly true in the case of ministers! The thought passed through my mind that some ministers' conferences might benefit from her presence in order that the sheep be distinguished from the goats!

In spite of all these strange symptoms however, the woman's intellectual powers remained unimpaired. Her state of possession had in fact only been brought about by her persistent practice of spiritism over a good number of years.

The phenomenon of resistance is not known among the mentally ill. In people like the Gadarene demoniac on the other hand, it is clearly visible. When he saw

Jesus he began to shout out, "What do you want with me? I adjure you not to torment me." This is the typical reaction of one possessed. In the Roman Catholic Missal one of the symptoms of possession is described as an aversion towards the things of God. Yes, even the Catholic Church is aware of the fact. Significantly too, Professor Bender of Freiburg University, a well-known parapsychologist, has also acknowledged the existence of the phenomenon of resistance, and in doing so gives indirect affirmation to the reality of the demonic.

This aversion, to the things of God is a common symptom of possessed people all over the world. It is an indication therefore, of the meta-physical and meta-medical situation which exists here. Possession is not primarily a disease of the mind. It is rather the influence, and sometimes even the indwelling, of evil spirits and powers. Therefore, the problem facing us is to be dealt with by the Christian worker rather than by the psychiatrist.

Of course one recognizes that there are many mental illnesses which have no connection whatever with the demonic. In fact one must be very careful indeed when one uses the word 'demonic' or the word 'possession.' There are far fewer people who are demon possessed than some primitive sects would have us believe. But conversely, there are far more people in the world today suffering from the effects of the demonic than our psychiatrists and modern theologians would care to admit. Both sides are guilty of false diagnoses. Yet I have heard several Christian psychiatrists in areas where occultism is rife, affirm that sometimes more than half the inmates of their psychiatric clinics are demonically oppressed rather than mentally ill.

Because demon possession and the demonic are such controversial subjects, to clarify our argument we will now go on to list some of the more important symptoms of possession in the narrower sense, where the demons actually indwell the person concerned.[2]

a) *Alteration of Voice.*

Let it be said, before we go on, that these symptoms do not occur in connection with genuine mental illnesses.

One clear way of recognising demon possession is by the alteration of the voice of the possessed person during the time of his or her attacks. I came across the following example during my counselling work in Brazil. The sister of a minister gave every appearance of being possessed. For many years she had lived with a Cabocla or, in other words, a spiritist. When the Cabocla had died the

---

[2]See Chapter 6.

woman who had been his mistress began to suffer from strange experiences. Sometimes she would fall into a trance and the Cabocla's voice would speak out of her. Simultaneously she would begin to walk and act like him too.

b)   *Clairvoyance.*

This second symptom is quite unique. It, too, occurs in the possessed person only during the time of the attacks. A vivid example of this was told me by a Mrs. Sutton in Port Elizabeth. When I was counselling her she told me several examples of her clairvoyant powers. She had once seen an upright coffin standing in her room. She had cried out in alarm. A few days later her 11 year old grandson had been killed in a motor car accident. Every time, in fact, a member of her family or someone in the neighborhood died she had had previous warning of the event. To some people this is just a case of second sight, but with possessed people it is a spontaneous experience which often happens when the evil spirits are in control. As I listened further to Mrs. Sutton's account of her life, the root of her oppression gradually came to light. Her grandfather, on his death bed, had transferred his magical powers to her. Ever since that time she had been demonically oppressed and controlled.

c) *Speaking in Foreign Languages.*

The most vivid distinguishing mark between a possessed person and someone merely suffering from a mental illness, is the ability to speak in a foreign language which the oppressed person has never learned before. I could quote quite a number of examples of this, including not a few of which I have had personal experience.

A missionary who had been working in Africa came back home to Zurich in Switzerland on furlough. One evening he was confronted by a possessed person. While in a trance the person had suddenly begun to speak in an African dialect which the missionary recognized as coming from the area in which he had worked. In his conscious state the possessed person did not know even a single word of the dialect in question.

In New Zealand a man became acquainted with a spiritistic medium. He took part in some table-lifting and discovered that while in a trance the medium was able to speak in a foreign language. Later, the New Zealander came to me for counselling. Since his first contact with the medium, he had begun to suffer from disturbances in his spiritual life.

It is interesting to note in passing that so-called speaking in tongues is not only a gift of the Holy Spirit but also a sign of demon possession. Moreover, there is also a psychological form of tongues speaking.

d) *Occult Transference.*

Another problem connected with possession is transference. It is true that a form of transference exists in the medical world of psychology and psychiatry, whereby a doctor or nurse who cares for the mentally sick can fall prey to the same disorder. I know, in fact, of two psychiatrists who as a result of their work, committed suicide. One was Professor Schneider of Heidelberg University, and the other a psychiatrist from Amsterdam. Occult transference, however, is of an entirely different nature. If mental illness is transferred from one person to another, the original patient is not cured as a result but continues to suffer from the disease. In possession, on the other hand, if the 'spiritual' doctor or nurse has the 'illness' transferred to them, the originally possessed person goes free. Let me illustrate this.

In Germany, a late friend of mine,

Fr. Heitmuller, was recognized by all to be a genuine man of God. One day another Christian had asked him to visit his demon possessed son. Heitmuller agreed to go along, but he took with him a teacher friend together with the teacher's own son. For several hours they prayed for the possessed boy, commanding the demons to leave in the Name of Jesus. Finally, after a long battle the boy was freed. But that was not all. That same afternoon, as the first boy was delivered, the teacher's son who had been present throughout the session himself became possessed. How, one might ask, could this have happened? It later came to light that the boy who was now possessed had not in fact been a genuine Christian. Heitmuller himself had not realized this before, otherwise he would never have allowed him to participate in the counselling session. This type of counselling should only be engaged in by Christians who have really been born again, who are continuing to live holy lives, and who place themselves under the blood of Jesus for protection.

Instantaneous Deliverance. [3]

Yet another clear distinction

_____
[3]See Chapter 6

between mental illness and possession
is the instantaneous deliverance of the
possessed person when he comes into
healing contact with Jesus. Psychiatrists can struggle for years with
schizophrenics, paranoids and manic
depressives with little, if any, improvement being observed. In the realm of
Christian counselling on the other
hand, sudden and continuous deliverance can and does take place. With the
Gadarene demoniac it only required a
word from Jesus - "Come out" - and
the possessed man was free. And He
whom the Son of God makes free is
free indeed!

XIII. *The Christian's Position.*

Let us sum up what we have been saying
with a few general observations.

A.   The question of the demonic covers a much
wider area than just possession. Pharisaism,
hypocrisy and pride, for example, can
cause a person to come under attack from
Satan's forces as well. We have only chosen
to speak about possession in order to illustrate the more general problem of demonic
subjection, and this it aptly does. What
then, we may ask, should our attitude be
towards the demonic as a whole?

1.   Some primitive Christian groups are prone
to read the demonic into almost everything
they cannot understand, organically-based

depressions and headaches included. However, the people who hold this attitude have been the source of a great deal of harm and confusion, and have brought much misery into the lives of many they have tried to counsel. One continually needs to warn people to avoid hastily labelling someone as being possessed. Personally speaking, I would never tell a person I thought he was possessed.

2. The opposite extreme of denying the existence of the demonic completely, is usually based on either ignorance, arrogance or both. There are many people of apparently superior intelligence who accuse anyone who believes in demonic possession of having a medieval attitude. But as Paul wrote: "God catches the wise by their own craftiness."

3. Between these two extremes one can take one of many attitudes. Let us therefore first listen to the words of the great Lutheran Christian, Hermann Bezzel, who said, "Mankind is demonized to the extent that it believes the demons do not exist!" Unfortunately today, many intellectuals, following the current trends in scientific and medical theory, believe possession to be an out-dated concept. Not only do modern theologians follow them in their error, but sometimes believing Christians do the same. I know for example, of the direc-

tor of a missionary society who dismissed one of his missionaries simply because he had tried to counsel a possessed man rather than send him to a psychiatrist.

4. There are other Christians, however, who, although they may believe in demons, still maintain that because Jesus was victorious on the cross we no longer need concern ourselves about such matters. The subject of the demonic is therefore banned from their teaching, and as a result, young preachers and missionaries coming from such schools of thought are wholly unprepared for the battle they meet on the field. The conflict I have had with such people who are often the leaders of our Bible Schools and seminaries, is really disheartening. I have illustrated this many times in my books.

    The closer we come to the return of our Lord, however, the harder the struggle will become. Yet the victory will be the Lord's. No matter what forces and schemes the devil may use, we must arm ourselves with the triumphant theme of the last book in the Bible. In the face of all the chaos looming on the horizon, we can raise our heads in confidence and cry, "Even so, come Lord Jesus."

5. There is another problem facing us today which is especially prevalent in the United States. It is that many Christians teach that

when one becomes a Christian all one's problems are solved. In answer to this idea I can only turn to the literally thousands of Christians who have come to me in counselling sessions, who have carried their occult subjection over with them into their Christian lives. It is true that with a deep conversion a person can be delivered from all such oppressions of the devil, but this does not often take place. This can be illustrated by a simple analogy. If a young man, for example, contracts venereal disease before he becomes a Christian, although as a result of turning to Christ his sins may be forgiven, the effect of his sins will nevertheless almost certainly remain. So it is with occultism. A person can quite easily carry the effects of either his own or his ancestors' sins of sorcery over into his Christian life. And it is a person like this who needs the counsel of an experienced Christian worker. It is shocking to find in our Bible Schools and training colleges that hardly any time is devoted to preparing intending Christian workers for the problems they will surely meet in this field.

Yet happily, there still are and have been a few men who are qualified to work amongst the demonically oppressed. Dr. V. Raymond Edman, the late chancellor of Wheaton College, clearly recognized the problem and suggested that I hold a series of lectures there to make the students aware of the various problems involved.

However, he died before this suggestion could be followed up. Do not misunderstand me. I am not looking for a job. I am simply pointing out the serious lack of training which is given to our future ministers and missionaries before they enter their life's work. It is like throwing a person into the deep end before he has learned to swim.

The need is growing every day wherever the demonic is being fought. Every Christian needs a suit of armor for both counsel and defence. A training in medicine and psychology can be very useful, but more important is the qualification of a converted life and a continuous state of growth. Equally one must have the authority of the Holy Spirit combined with the gift of discernment before one thinks of entering the fray. Maturity is also a factor which should not be lacking. Young Christians should hesitate before they enter the arena. It is best to take the advice and guidance of one's elder brothers and not rush in where angels fear to tread. In my own work among those who need this type of counsel, for many years now I have never even attempted to put one step forward without first ensuring that there has been a team of Christians praying behind me.

Our last word, though, is one of confidence. The Lord himself has promised to be with us and to protect us. Therefore we can go forward in faith, following the One who declared in Luke 10:19: "See, I have given you the authority to tread on serpents and scorpions and over all the power of the enemy, and nothing shall in any wise hurt you."

Chapter 3

MEDIUMISTIC POWERS, NATURAL POWERS AND SPIRITUAL GIFTS

(An address given at a Missionary Conference in Sydney, Australia.)

Summary

   I. Natural Powers
  II. The Gifts of the Holy Spirit
 III. Mediumistic Abilities
 IV. Characteristics:
     A.   Natural Gifts at Birth
     B.   Spiritual Gifts and the New Birth
     C.   Mediumistic Powers
  V. The Danger of Mediumistic Powers
     A.   The Argument of Scripture
     B.   The Argument of Origin
         1.   Inheritance
         2.   Transference
         3.   Occult Practices
     C.   Arguments from the Mission Field
     D.   The Experience of Christians
 VI. Christians and Mediumistic Abilities
VII. The Source of Deliverance

MEDIUMISTIC POWERS, NATURAL POWERS AND SPIRITUAL GIFTS

Let us begin by trying to explain the concepts before us, starting with the one which is least difficult to define.

I. *Natural Powers.*

Without realizing it, we are surrounded by various powers and forces immediately after we enter this life. As young children we have to learn to live at peace with the force of gravity, with the laws which govern water, fire, wind and electricity. At school we are led on to grasp the rudiments of other physical and chemical forces. We learn about the power within the atom, the forces which hold the universe and the solar system together, facts which we can behold but which we are still a long way from really understanding. More recently we have heard of other forces, the power of the laser for example. And who knows, maybe it is this and not the power of the atom which holds the key to future world domination.

But this is only half the picture. What about the power which enables a gifted sculptor to see a finished statue of Christ within a rough unhewn piece of stone? What of the power which inspires a Beethoven, a Michelangelo or a Leonardo da Vinci?

Yet all these forces and abilities lie within the natural sphere. It is true that they can be put to either good or ill effect, but fundamentally they are neutral and natural in character. This neutral characteristic, however, is conditional and not absolute. It is forever overshadowed and influenced by two other domains. Man is too weak to maintain his neutrality in the face of these transcendental powers. If we believe that we are master of our gifts, then we are wrong. We are already in the hands of another power far greater than ourselves (1 Cor. 12; Rom. 12; Eph. 2).

II.   *The Gifts of the Holy Spirit.*

Turning to the concept of spiritual gifts we find that the New Testament draws a clear line between charismata and ordinary intellectual gifts, even when the natural gifts are those of a Goethe or an Einstein.

Spiritual gifts are in fact the gifts of the Holy Spirit. They are therefore wholly unrelated to human nature. They stem rather from the divine nature, from the Holy of Holies itself. They are characteristics of the Holy Spirit which are not to be found in natural unregenerate man. They come to us from above by grace after the rebirth, and far from being ours by right can be taken back if God so chooses.

In 1 Corinthians 12 we find the following gifts listed by the apostle Paul: wisdom, the wisdom of the Holy Spirit and not human wisdom; knowledge; faith; gifts of healing; the working of miracles; prophecy; the discerning of spirits; diverse kinds of tongues; the interpretation of tongues — nine gifts. Strangely enough the greatest gift is not mentioned in this context. In Romans 5:5, however, Paul describes how that "the love of God is spread abroad in our heart by the Holy Spirit", and at the end of 1 Corinthians 12, although he writes that we should covet the best gifts, he adds, "and yet I show you a more excellent way . . ."

Having presented us with this challenge, Paul then goes on to devote a whole chapter to love, thus confirming that love is the highest of all spiritual gifts as well as the chief of the fruits of the Holy Spirit (Gal. 5).

III. *Mediumistic Abilities.*

There is a lot of controversy surrounding the idea of mediumistic abilities. Even amongst Christian workers there is a good deal of disunity and ignorance. I have met some ministers and even evangelists who have either used a pendulum or been treated by occult practitioners for years without realizing that anything was wrong.

Before explaining the exact character of mediumistic abilities let me first describe how I have collected the material on which I base my opinion. For the past 40 years I have kept a file of all those whose occult problems I have had to deal with, both personally and through correspondence, and whose experiences have increased my insight on the subject. But as Paul wrote, "We only know in part." I am well aware therefore of the limitation of my own knowledge, and the corresponding responsibility on my shoulders to give a correct assessment of mediumistic forces.

First of all then let us explain what we mean by 'mediumistic'. The word is derived from the Latin word 'medium'. A medium is a person who acts as a mediator, someone who makes contact between two parties, between the human level and other-worldly powers.

Mediumistic faculties themselves are not the possession of everyone, nor are they under the control of a person's normal consciousness.

Just as we have given a list of spiritual gifts, so we can give a list of mediumistic abilities. As in the case of charismata, so with mediumistic powers, we can name some ten to twenty different types. Among others they include: clairvoyance; clairsentience; clairaudience; sensitivity to the rod and pendulum telepathy, although traces of natural telepathy also exist; trance states, especially in spiritism; excursion of the soul, practiced especially by the Rosicrucians; mesmerism, although this too exists in a natural form; mental suggestion in its occult form; telekinesis or psychokinesis.

These mediumistic abilities can be divided into two groups, one passive and the other active: perception and influence. Parapsychologists speak of Psi-gamma and Psi-kappa phenomena, 'psi' standing for extrasensory phenomena, 'gamma' coming from the Greek word 'gignoskein' meaning 'to know', and 'kappa' from the Greek word 'kinein', meaning 'to move'. It is interesting to see the connection here with the story of the temptation in Genesis chapter 3: to be like God, having His power, knowing good from evil. The whole range of mediumistic abilities is concerned in fact with knowledge and power.

IV.   *Characteristics.*

The next question we must ask ourselves concerns the characteristics of these powers. We need spend no time, however, describing what we have called natural powers. Suffice it to say that these powers can either be placed at God's service or at the service of Satan.

The real question facing us is how we are to differentiate between and assess mediumistic abilities and spiritual gifts. We must approach this problem one step at a time, seeing in each case how the various gifts are received.

A.   As we have already intimated, natural gifts are present at birth, and have merely to be developed during the process of growing up.

B.   Spiritual gifts, on the other hand, are given to us after rebirth, when we are born again of the Holy Spirit. Sometimes they are like seedlings which need to be nurtured. For example, Paul wrote to Timothy, his fellow worker, "Do not neglect the gift you have, which was given to you by prophecy, when the elders laid their hands upon you" (1 Tim. 4:14). The spiritual father of these gifts is the Holy Spirit. No follower of Jesus has been left emptyhanded at his spiritual rebirth. But the gifts often have to be awakened. Nevertheless they are there, so long as our spiritual life is genuine and has been born of the Spirit of God.

Some of God's children believe that they have no spiritual gifts. But to believe this is almost to insult God himself. Why? Let me give an example. If, on the reading of his father's will, the eldest son discovered that he had been disinherited, wouldn't he be justified in criticizing his father on this account? The same would be true if our heavenly father disinherited us. As disciples of Christ therefore, is it conceivable that our Father has disinherited us? Never. If the Holy Spirit has caused us to be born into the family of God then we will not be born emptyhanded. We must count on these gifts and pray that the Holy Spirit will reveal them to us in our lives.

We are not God's step-children. He has not disowned us. No, we are the heirs of the richest Father in the universe.

C. But where do mediumistic gifts and abilities come from? And what characterizes them? Some theologians and parapsychologists claim that these abilities are neutral, but with this I cannot agree. It is true that there is possibly a small strip of neutral telepathy apart from its occult form, and the same may be the case for clairsentience, mesmerism and mental suggestion. As far as I have observed, however, in thousands of cases, mediumism is invariably of a demonic character. The reason for this may be that the devil always uses a natural disposition for mediumism as an open door for his own influence, to create centers of demonic power in numerous people's lives. And I do not say this lightly, but base my observations on the evidence of many years' study.

V. *The Danger of Mediumistic Powers*

A. The Bible consistently associates occultism and sorcery with mediumistic abilities. We can see this in Deuteronomy 18:10-12, and in Leviticus 20:6, 20:27, for example. In Acts 16 Paul also calls the mediumistic power of the girl fortune-teller demonic. In the light of this it is not right to regard these abilities as a new field for scientific research, and still less as the gifts of God.

B. Further evidence of their evil nature can be seen in the way in which they originate. This occurs in one of three ways: through heredity, transference, or occult experimentation.

1. Through investigating the background of numerous families in which mediumistic abilities are in evidence, I have discovered that when someone has the ability to use a pendulum or to practice mesmerism, one can predict with almost absolute certainty that he has had either a grandparent or a great-grandparent who has practiced magic

charming. Magical charmers have descendants in the third and fourth generation who are mediumistically endowed. It is a fulfilment of the second commandment: "I will visit the iniquity of the fathers on the children to the third and fourth generation of those that hate me."

It is true that such mediumistic abilities are not a sin in themselves to the one who inherits them, but they are a burden. The Swiss Christian, Markus Hauser, who carried such abilities himself, freely admitted this.

Many times I have been told by Christians that when a person is converted he loses any mediumistic abilities that he may previously have had. This, however, is simply not true, but we will deal with this problem a little later.

2. Another way of receiving mediumistic abilities is through occult transference. If someone with the ability to use a rod or pendulum holds the hands of a person without the ability, a transference can take place which surprisingly is permanent. Transferred powers, however, are never as strong as inherited ones.

3. Thirdly, mediumism can be caused by a person taking an active part in occultism. Curiosity can lead a person to read occult literature and to experiment on his own.

During the course of such experimentation mediumistic abilities can develop.

Again this illustrates quite clearly our thesis that mediumistic powers come from the nether world rather than from above.

C. Further evidence of the demonic nature of mediumistic abilities is seen in their close connection with the pagan rites of primitive tribes. There is an ominous connection between the mediumistic powers one finds in Europe and the magical practices of primitive tribes throughout the world. I can quote two almost identical examples to illustrate this.

Whilst in the Philippines I came across the so-called Hilot, the magicians of the islands. One of their chiefs, Datu by name, had a special reputation. He could make his hand become so hot that an egg could be cooked upon it. When this man became a Christian, however, he was in no doubt that his abilities were of a demonic nature.

And now the sequel from Germany. I was holding a mission in the town of Husum, in the north of Germany, when the minister told me about a member of his congregation who had what he called 'a hot hand'. He described too, how the man had healed numerous people. The healer attended the church's men's group, and the minister felt that his gift had been given him by God. Personally, I could not accept this, especially as the whole district was riddled with occult practices. Moreover the man himself was not a genuine Christian. One of the problems in Germany today is that people think that they are Christians merely because they attend one or two church services per week.

No, the Hilot from the Philippines and the healer from Germany were both in possession of the same mediumistic power.

Let me quote another parallel to this.

In Hawaii the men who practice black magic are called Kahunas. These people can inflict a disease on another person, even over a distance, by means of their mediumistic abilities. In America and Europe in so-called Christian countries similar things take place. A woman came to me complaining that since leaving the Christian Science Movement she had been persecuted by the negative use of mental suggestion. Let me point out that it was Mary Baker Eddy herself who described this art in one of her books. Talking about a process called malpractice, she described how it can be used to either mentally or magically persecute people one wants to attack.

Whether it is a Kahuna or a malpracticing Christian Scientist, the power at work is the same. The only difference is that in Hawaii the power is clearly pagan, while in the West it is dressed up with Christian trimmings.

Another indication of the true nature

of mediumistic powers is seen in the effects these powers have on the mission field. The people who most resist the Christian message are almost invariably those possessing mediumistic abilities. Added to this, if these mediumistic people ever do come to Christ, they recognize at once the true nature of their former powers. It is only in the so-called Christian world that the boundaries are blurred. This is sometimes the result of a corresponding blurring of what true faith really is. Often Christian tradition is mistaken for Christian life. Church membership is confused with discipleship. These are dangerous presuppositions. People become regarded as Christians merely if they are congenially disposed towards the Church, even when they are burdened by the strongest occult subjections.

Mediumistic powers act as a block to one's spiritual life. If one investigates the life and work of any missionary who uses the pendulum, for example, you will be sure to find that it has in fact weakened his ministry. Mediumistic powers paralyze spiritual power. I could not give only one but hundreds of examples to illustrate this fact.

D.   Lastly we turn to the actual experience of believers concerning the nature of mediumistic powers.

In Bietigheim, for example, there is a well-known Christian diviner. Many people

give him money in return for the service he
offers. He told me, however, when I talked
with him, that when he has searched for
water he cannot pray properly for days.
During this time, if he wants to read the
Bible he gets spots before the eyes. If he
hears a person preaching the Word of God
he cannot concentrate at all, however hard
he tries.

Another example comes from
Freiburg. I was holding a series of meetings
there when I was suddenly taken ill. I went
and visited a doctor, but on seeing a
pendulum hanging up in his consulting
room I felt I had to leave immediately.
However, on this occasion the Lord gave
me the inner liberty to say to the doctor,
"You can use your pendulum on me if you
want to." I had never allowed such a thing
before in all my life. Inwardly I was
praying that God would have his way in the
matter. If he wanted the pendulum to work
or if he wanted to stop it from working, I
would leave the matter in his hands The
pendulum did not react. The doctor tried it
in several places in the room. Still it would
not work. Finally he remarked, "Well,
you're the first person it hasn't worked
on." It was then that I told him what I had
been asking God to do. The doctor reacted
with extreme honesty. "If that's the case,"
he said, "then I won't use a pendulum any
more in my practice." Later I discovered
that he had kept his promise. Let me say,

though, before we go on, that nobody should copy what I did in this circumstance. Unless God commissions us to act in this way the results could well be fatal.

A Christian was having a house built in Gebweiler in France. Because there was no main water-supply to the house, his brother sent for a water diviner without his knowledge to help discover if there was a natural source of water on his land. When the Christian realized this, he knelt down and prayed, "Lord, if this man's power is not from you then stop it working. If on the other hand you've given him his ability then let him be successful in looking for water." Having prayed he went out into the garden. To his surprise he was greeted by swearing, followed by the words, "What's wrong with it? I found water here a moment ago, and now it won't work." The diviner's power had been blocked. The Christian's prayer had been answered.

A power which can be driven away by prayer is not a power or a gift of God. Neither is it a harmless natural gift. No, such forces are opposed to the work of God and should be avoided at all costs.

VI. *Christians and Mediumistic Abilities.*

We come now to the most difficult problem of all. As we have seen in our investigation, sometimes even believing Christians can possess or be carriers of mediumistic abilities. But if, as I have already indicated, mediumistic abilities are the result of sins to do with sorcery, it seems to be contrary to common sense that Christians should be plagued by these faculties. Let us therefore examine the problem further.

Let me tell you a story which underlines the principles I feel are involved here. A young man much addicted to alcohol was prone to violence in his drunken state, often threatening the people about him with his knife. One evening another man took offence to his attitude and, drawing a stiletto dagger, stabbed him in the back. The young man was seriously wounded and forced to remain in the hospital for some months. Through the witness of a Christian nurse on the ward, he was converted. Immediately he was freed from his alcoholic addiction and evil behaviour and he found forgiveness of sins. Despite his new birth though, his wounds remained, and he has had to carry them with him ever since. Yes, it is true that we are forgiven, but the injuries and damage done by past sins often remain.

Let me quote another example. An alcoholic has had his health destroyed through drink. He is the father of several children. Then he meets Christ and is freed from his sin and from his former evil habits. But his children are not freed from the consequences of their father's alcoholism and inherit the effects in their own lives. Examples like these occur by the thousands.

Now we can turn to the question of mediumistic powers. It is true that in some cases of conversion the depth of experience is so great that all the effects of the person's former life of sin and any inherited mediumistic abilities are gone for ever. But there are also many conversions in which in spite of the confessing person receiving forgiveness of sins, his mediumistic abilities remain, albeit sometimes unconsciously. But one thing must immediately be stressed. Any Christian who knows he is mediumistically disposed and who asks the Lord to deliver him, will be truly set free. God is no man's debtor. But many people do not know that they are subjected in this way and that their spiritual lives are burdened or obstructed. Some even think that their mediumistic ability is a gift of God. This is a dangerous mistake indeed.

The problem becomes even more alarming when one realizes that the following series of events often occurs. A man who was formerly a spiritist is converted. He is forgiven and receives eternal life, but his mediumistic abilities remain. Now as a Christian he draws on these abilities and lays hands on people and prays for people, not realising that his laying on of hands is extremely dangerous for those on whom it is performed.

A Christian should never use mediumistic abilities in the service of the Lord. He should pray rather that the Lord remove them and replace them with the gifts of the Holy Spirit. To argue that they can now be used for good ends because the person has become a Christian is false. The Holy Spirit never joins himself to that which has been won from the realms of occultism and sorcery. This is clear from the

story of the girl in Acts 16. Mediumistic forces,
no matter how they may be dressed with Christian trimmings, are of the devil and not of God.

As a last resort someone might ask, as
many missionaries have indeed done so, "If we
find ourselves in a drought, for example, and
need water urgently, would it still be wrong to
call in the help of a diviner?" What can one say
to this objection?

There are three permissible ways of search-
ing for water. One can try drilling; one can use
scientific instruments like the protone resonance
magnetometer — but both these methods are
rather expensive; or the Christian can use prayer.
Indeed far from being the last resort, he should
pray before he tries anything else. Did not Jesus
teach us to pray for 'our daily bread'? If he can
give the children of Israel water in the wilderness, or supply Hagar with a spring in the desert,
how much more can he give us the things we
need!

Like denying our faith, it would be better
to die of thirst than to resort to mediumistic
powers and the power of the devil in order to
remain alive.

Let me give you just one more example on
this subject. In the summer of 1971 I was present at a ministers' seminar at North Platte in
Nebraska. The seminar had been arranged by
Clifton McElheran and about 60 to 70 ministers
were present. We were engaged in a discussion
on the use of the divining rod when Mrs.
McElheran stood up and gave the following
wonderful testimony. I have her permission to

publish it for the sake of other Christian workers.

Mrs. McElheran and her husband had worked for the Sudan Interior Mission in Africa. On many of the mission stations they learned that there was a lack of water, and this in turn led Mrs. McElheran to the discovery of her own ability to divine. Many of the missionaries used her services, but as time progressed she found that her nervous system was becoming increasingly burdened. This resulted in her returning home six months earlier than had been planned. She was so weak at the time that she had to be confined to bed. The doctor was unable to discover the cause of her illness. Then one day a friend of her husband brought her my book 'Between Christ and Satan'. She read the first chapter on the divining rod with interest. Her eyes were immediately opened. Going out into the garden with her own rod she found a place where the rod was drawn down strongly in her hands. She stopped, and then prayed, "Lord, if this ability is not from you, then take it away." She took the rod and tried again. Nothing happened. Her prayer had been answered. Breaking the rod in pieces she repented and asked God to forgive her and to deliver her from the effects of her sin. And God graciously did just that. Her ability to divine has never returned.

Summing up, we repeat that as Christians we can freely use the gifts which God decides to give us as well as any help we can obtain from the scientific world, but mediumistic forces and abilities must be avoided at all costs seeing that they originate from the sins of sorcery of either ourselves or our ancestors.

VII. *The Source of Deliverance.*

The first and the last person to whom we as Christians should turn for help is the God and Father of our Lord Jesus Christ, to the Lord Jesus himself, and to the Holy Spirit whom He has sent. Matthias Claudius put it this way:

We build castles in the sky,

Our hands at many things try,

yet we drift further from the goal.

It is strange how children of God try almost everything before turning to God for all that they need.

But now I want to give an example where we can see the Holy Spirit's gift of miracles clearly and visibly at work. The incident took place in Egypt. A simple peasant woman who could neither read nor write became a Christian. She began to attend the Egyptian Coptic Church, but her one sorrow was that she was unable to read the New Testament for herself. In childlike faith she prayed unceasingly that God would teach her how to read. One night she saw in a vision a hand which gave her a red copy of the New Testament. And in the vision she found she could actually read its contents. A little while after this her dream began to come true and she was given a red New Testament just like the one in the vision. She prayed after receiving it and then bent over it to look at the words. Suddenly her eyes began to understand the meaning of the words she saw. Within a short space of time she could read the book without difficulty. But the miracle only applied to the New Testament. She still could not read other books or newspapers. To judge the story with our rational minds would be to sit back, smile and say, "Well it sounds very nice." Some day God is going to hold us responsible for and judge us for the supercilious attitude we so often adopt.

We have a God who can still work miracles today. The Lord who fed the 5,000 with a handful of loaves and fishes is the Lord of the twentieth century. He can help each and every one of his children no matter how small the offering they bring to him to bless. As David sang:

> "I will lift my eyes to the hills.
> From whence does my help come?
> My help comes from the Lord,
> who made heaven and earth!"

If we are willing to yield ourselves to Him completely, to become broken, then we will become partakers of the miracle-working power of the Holy Spirit. To desire this power is not to fall into the trap into which Adam fell. No, it is to obey the voice of the Lord Who through His written Word commands us to turn to Him and accept His divine power through which we can become partakers of the divine nature.

Chapter 4

OCCULT SUBJECTION, THE NEGLECTED FACTOR IN MENTAL ILLNESSES

(An address given at the Medical Centre in Seoul, Korea.)

Summary

I. Introduction
II. Psychical Abnormalities
    A.   Medicine
    B.   Psychiatry
    C.   Psychotherapy
III. Oppressions with Unknown Causes
IV. Examples from Counselling Work
V. Parapsychology and Occultism
VI. The Effects of Occult Practices
VII. Our Commission

OCCULT SUBJECTION, THE NEGLECTED FACTOR IN MENTAL ILLNESSES

I. *Introduction*

To introduce the subject I will begin by quoting an example. Let me first say though that although most of the examples I will be quoting will be cases involving the medical profession, there will be no confessional or professional confidences broken in the process.

The medical superintendent of two psychiatric institutions asked me to give a few lectures to his staff. I agreed and was subsequently drawn into some heated discussions with them. I was introduced to a number of the patients at the institutions, the superintendent commenting that their symptoms failed to fit into the normal framework of psychiatric illnesses. His statement highlights one of the distinguishing marks of occult subjection in fact, for it is very difficult to square its symptoms with those of normal mental ilnesses. Anyway, continuing with our example, one of the patients who was introduced to me was a former doctor who had been admitted to the asylum a number of years before. It was one of his better days and he was able to talk to me freely. His wife is a Christian and his father an almost world-famous doctor. The superintendent had already informed me that they did not really know what was wrong with the man, in spite of having had him under observation for a considerable time. However, during my conversation with him I was able to obtain some clues which psychiatrists had either overlooked or regarded as seemingly unimportant factors. The doctor had had a secretary who had been a practicing medium. When he had discovered this, he had shown an interest in her spare-time 'occupation' and had begun to make her the subject of some experiments. It was during this time that his depressions and other mental disturbances first appeared. The more he had become involved in these spiritistic experiments, the more his condition had deteriorated. It was as a result of this that he was finally admitted to the mental institution. It was not surprising to me that the psychiatrists had been unable to help him. Whether or not he had a genuine psychosis, it was absolutely clear from my point of view that he was also occultly oppressed. No one can enter and leave a spiritistic laboratory unpunished. As Professor Hauter of Strasbourg University said to his students after he himself had participated in some spiritistic seances, "No one comes out unplucked. Everybody has got to lose some feathers!"

Well, so much for our first example. The question we are therefore faced with is, can we attempt to tackle cases of oppression such as this with the tools of medical science?

II.   *Psychical Abnormalities.*

When a patient with mental or psychical abnormalities seeks our professional help, either as a Christian counsellor or as a medical doctor, we naturally try to diagnose his complaint correctly and give him the therapy he needs. To do this properly we need to take into consideration all the auxiliary sciences which might apply to his particular problem. In this respect there are essentially three branches of science which can supply us with tools designed to combat and cure mental disorders. These are:

A.   Medicine,
B.   Psychiatry,
C.   The Psychological sciences such as psychotherapy and depth-psychology.

It would be too much to go into each of these fields in detail, so we must be content with just a brief summary of what they involve.

A.   *Medicine.*

The connection between the body and the mind is being increasingly recognized by doctors today. A number of organic diseases are now known to have definite psychical side-effects. Jaundice, for example, is known to be able to cause depression. Heart diseases, as for example angina pectoris, myomalacia cordis (myocardiopathy), myodegeneratio cordis (myocardial degenerative disease) and paroxysmal tachycardia, can all produce disorders of the mind. A thyroid gland that fails to function correctly can also bring on depressions. A low calcium concentration in the blood can produce visionary experiences, and a low hormone concentration can produce a severe depressive state. Various poisons can similarly bring on depressions. These facts are just a few known to those who specialize in internal medicine. One could go on to mention the mental effect produced sometimes by over-dieting. I know of the case of a certain minister who committed suicide after losing 36 pounds through a radical diet, in spite of having no previous history of mental depression. It seems quite likely that his mental collapse was the direct result of his loss of weight. It hardly needs mentioning too, that many drug addicts during the various stages of withdrawal pass through states of severe mental distress.

B. *Psychiatry.*

In the field of psychiatry, German psychiatrists recognize some five different methods of treatment for mental disease. These are: 1. The use of drugs which effect the subconscious, including Megaphen, Serpacil, Tofranil, Nardil, Neurocil and so on; 2. Electric shock treatment (E.C.T.); 3. Continuous sleep treatment; 4. Continuous hydropathic treatment, a method which is currently gaining ground in America; 5. Life-cell injections. In America another method called 'group therapy' has been developed over the last few years. An increasing number of psychiatrists are also coming to the opinion that schizophrenia, one of the commonest forms of mental illness, is caused through a change in the chemistry of the brain, and experiments have been conducted by doctors like Dr. Hoffer and Dr. Osmond, to see if schizophrenia can actually be cured by using niacin. Indeed astonishing successes have been obtained through the daily administration of niacin to patients. There is still some scepticism about this method, however, amongst other doctors and psychiatrists.

My main objection to these forms of treatment, and I base this objection on hundreds of personal observations, is that many so-called schizophrenics are not really suffering from schizophrenia at all, but are suffering instead from some form of occult or demonic oppression. I realize, however, that many people will react strongly to a statement like this.

C.   *Psychotherapy.*

One of the subjects studied by the psychological sciences is abnormal developments in a person's character from early childhood onwards. In Europe the young science of psychotherapy or psychopathology is closely connected with the names of Freud, Adler and Jung. The actual therapy suggested by those who specialize in this field is psychoanalysis. Dream interpretation by means of free association, and narcotherapy are also used. In America another method of treatment is that known by the name of psychodrama. This is advocated particularly where exaggerated attitudes of antagonism or defence exist. The patient is asked to act the part, for instance, of a son who feels embittered against his father, and then the roles are changed, and the one acting the son is asked to take the father's part, and vice versa. The aim is to help the patients to a mutual understanding of one another's problems and thereby to heal the traumas (wounds) of the subconscious from which they are suffering.

So ends our extremely brief sketch of the various medical and psychological sciences which one must consider when treating those who suffer either mentally, or spiritually, or both.

III. *Oppressions With Unknown Causes.*

Having considered the methods used by the medical world, we are still left with the question, what is our approach to a person whose illness or state of mind is not covered by the above mentioned branches of science? Let me just outline a few factors not normally dealt with by these sciences as a whole.

A. A few years ago a book was published with the provocative title "30 Years Among the

Dead". The author was a Swedish psychiatrist, and although I cannot agree with his main thesis based as it is on spiritistic lines, the book does in fact make one very important point. The author writes that many people who are regarded as mentally ill, are in reality demon possessed. As I have said, in spite of the man being a spiritist I must agree with him here.

B. A second statement worth bearing in mind comes from a Christian psychiatrist who reported that about 60% of the patients at the asylum where he worked were either demonized or possessed, rather than mentally ill!

C. Thirdly, I would refer you back to the example I quoted at the beginning of my talk. The superintendent of the two clinics stated quite plainly that the patient's symptoms failed to agree with the known pattern of mental disorders.

D. Fourthly, Dr. Lechler, who was the medical superintendent of the largest clinic for nervous diseases in Germany, not only believes in demonic subjection but even differentiates between four degrees of oppression; namely, occult subjection, demonization, obsession, and finally, possession.

Yet it is almost impossible to talk about demons and possession in the terms

of medical science. We are therefore forced
to leave the scientific approach behind us
and move over into the world of meta-
physics. Let me state again then, that
occult subjection and possession are not so
much medical terms as spiritual/religious
terms. It is therefore the business of the
Christian worker rather than the psychiatrist to overcome this source of suffering in
the world.

The difference between mental illness
and possession is most clearly seen by com-
paring their symptoms. I think that the
best way in which I can do this therefore, is
to quote a few examples.

In France a young minister rang up a
doctor and asked him to come quickly
because a young woman in his parish had
suddenly gone raving mad. The minister's
modernist views prevented him from believing in Satan, or demons or anything like
possession and occult subjection. The
doctor on the other hand — I know him
well — was a real Christian. Following the
phone call he went to see the woman, and
on entering the house he prayed, as he
always did, that God would be with him
and show him how to deal with the patient.
He then gave her an injection to try and
calm her down. It had no effect. Half an
hour later therefore he gave her an injection of morphine. But again it had
no effect. He repeated the dose four
times within the next two hours but the

woman seemed to be as excited as she had been when he arrived. Turning to the minister the doctor finally said, "You know, this isn't mental illness. She's demon possessed! If she was suffering from a mental disorder the sedative would have taken effect by now. It's only in cases of possession that it has no effect." The doctor knew this from experience. He did not make the statement lightly.

There is another type of example which I have met several times personally. When a person who is mentally ill sits in front of me and I pray with him, there is never any change in his behaviour. He remains calm and composed throughout the prayer. On the other hand, if the person I am counselling is either demonized or possessed, when I begin to pray with him he reacts immediately with screams and curses and blasphemous words. The reaction is entirely different from those who are only pathologically ill. And possessed people always react in this way. Whenever they come into contact with the kingdom of God, be it through counselling or spiritual care, the resistance is always the same. Let it be noted that the reaction occurs even if the possessed person is unaware that he is being prayed for, when for example the people praying for him are in another room. He will begin to rave and fume just as if the people were present. The forces at work may be invisible to us but their effects can be clearly seen.

A second difference between occult and mental oppression is to be found in occult transference, although a form of transference is also known to exist in the medical and psychological world.

The simplest form of transference, familiar to us all, is seen in a child's urge to imitate its elders. If, however, this urge becomes excessive, or abnormal, it develops into an imitation neurosis.

Sometimes transference is also found in the psychoanalyst's consulting room. The patient can become personally dependent upon the doctor during the treatment, to such an extent that phases of rebellion, love and hate may arise, which have to be destroyed before any help can be achieved.

In the occult world, however, the form which transference takes is on a different plane altogether. I can illustrate this with an example. I know of a young Christian who prayed a great deal for her demonized girl friend. As a result, the demonized girl was healed, but the first girl became occultly subjected instead. But what is the difference between the two types of transference? With induced insanity, the person who is mentally ill is not cured, although his illness may be transferred to a doctor, or nurse, who is caring for him. In occult transference on the other hand, when transference takes place, the subjected person is always delivered, while the one who prays for him, or counsels him, is subjected instead. Numerous examples could be quoted in support of this statement, but I will mention only one.

A Christian worker opened his home to some occultly oppressed people in order to try and care for them and pray for them. In the end, however, his own son became demon possessed as a result of his contact with one of the patients. The Christian was forced to change his practice, and he allowed no more oppressed or demonized people to stay at his house. One can find no counterpart to this phenomenon in either medicine or psychology.

The greatest difference, however, between psychosis (mental illness) and occult subjection is the ability of a possessed person to speak in a foreign language while in a state of trance. This is not to be confused with genuine glossolalia, a gift of the Holy Spirit. It is rather a demonic counterpart to speaking in tongues. I know of both witch doctors and spiritistic mediums who are able to speak in foreign languages while in ecstasies or in a trance. I can give you an example of this from Australia. A missionary friend of mine with whom I once worked, told me of an incident he knew about where six tribal witch doctors, following a long ceremonious procedure, finally began to speak in foreign languages with voices not their own.

If I had the time I could go on to describe further characteristic differences between psychoses and possession. The conflict one meets with possessed people involve realms which transcend rational thought and understanding.

Let us not forget, however, that at the moment we are not so much dealing with the matter of proof, as presenting some of the evidence and signs. One cannot make God or the devil the subject of one's experiments. Their existence can only be illustrated by the effects they have on the world, an effect which the Bible clearly recognizes when it talks about the works of God and the works of Satan.

IV. *Examples from Counselling work.*

The following are some examples I have come across myself which I hope will give you a clearer insight into the characteristics of occult phenomena.

The first I will quote concerns a medical doctor with a large practice who came to see me on a number of occasions in order to receive spiritual help and counsel. He gave me his permission to publish his story as fully as I wished. This doctor had been in the habit of using a ouija-board to assist him in diagnosing the diseases of his patients. The ouija-board consists of a disc with the letters of the alphabet written round its circumference and the numbers 1 to 10 forming a smaller concentric circle. The instrument is widely used in Canada and the United States as a party game. When the doctor wished to know something about his patients he would hold a pendulum over the centre of the disc and then proceed to ask it questions. In response to his questions the pendulum would swing to and fro over the letters and numbers making up the answer. He had been so successful that the ouija-board had told him almost everything he had wanted to know. Apart from his medical work he could also ascertain the times of departures of trains, discover the name, age, address and profession of a person whose photograph he laid on the disc, and even at times predict future events like the result of elections and so on. However, as time went on the doctor became suspicious of his 'hobby'. He started to wonder what force lay behind it all. When he finally came to see me he confessed that while he had been using the ouija-board he had developed a violent temper, become addicted to both tobacco and alcohol, started suffering from depressions and begun to fear that he was going mad. Altogether I spent four counselling sessions with him trying to help him in his distress. In the end he relinquished his ouija-board and the occult literature he had collected, repented of his sin, and handed his life over to Christ. A small prayer group was formed at this time to pray for him, and this they continued to do over a period of months. In the end he was completely freed from his former afflictions and is today an ardent witness to the dangers of the ouija-board and the pendulum, as well as to the saving power of Christ.

I am well aware of the objection that many in the medical profession may raise concerning the confusion of the cause with the effect. When one realizes, however, the numerous other examples which can be quoted in support of this, the objection can be overruled.

Another case involves a person suffering from a pronounced compulsion neurosis. A young woman, 28 years old, came to me to be counselled. She had been undergoing psychiatric and psychotherapeutic treatment for a number of years but without avail. Her compulsion to wash herself, to count things, and to eat, still remained. She was in a terrible state. Her compulsion to eat was so strong that she would continue stuffing food into her mouth until she was sick, only to start all over again. When she finished her story I asked her if she had had any contact with spiritism. "Yes," she replied, "both my mother and my grandmother are very active spiritists. They often took me along to spiritistic meetings when I was a child."

Many people, on hearing a case like this for the first time, find it difficult to believe that there is any relationship between occult practices and the development of a neurosis. Suffice it to say, however, that in more than 50% of the neurotic people I have dealt with, this relationship has been present. Every psychiatrist knows how long and often futile the treatment of a neurosis can be. But why this? Because one of the most frequent causes of the complaint is not recognized by the medical profession. An incorrect diagnosis leads to the wrong treatment. A large proportion of neurotic people instead of consulting a psychiatrist should go to a Christian counsellor. But it would be wrong to generalize. I do not claim to have found the excelsior stone. Depressions and neuroses can occur in anything up to twenty different forms, and occult subjection is the cause of only one of these. However, among the millions of people suffering from neurotic illness in the world today, there must be hundreds of thousands who are suffering as a result of some occult subjection. Because our psychiatrists and psychologists continue to maintain that metaphysical influences simply do not exist, every one of these people receives the wrong therapy for his particular complaint. Every form of disease can be explained on a purely imminent basis, so the rationalist maintains, but in voicing this inhibition of his — philosophically it would be called an 'a priori' definition — he reveals that he is in the position neither to recognize nor to treat those depressions and neuroses which are caused by occultism. Many specialists are therefore simply of no use in this field, their university education having closed their eyes to one of the factors involved.

A few years ago at the Congress of Psychiatrists and Psychotherapists in Vienna, an American psychiatrist declared, "We are still only at the very beginning of our knowledge of the soul or psyche of man. Surgery is still in a far more advanced state than psychiatry." Statements like this help us to realize that there is still much virgin land waiting to be discovered when it comes to our knowledge of the workings of the human mind. One wonders why, therefore, we are not humble enough to admit this ignorance more often. Such an attitude might open many doors to future research. The mind and soul of man is the most precious part of God's creation. Why then do we so often ignore our Creator when it comes to the treatment of this most hallowed part of man?

V. *Parapsychology and Occultism.*

Let us turn our attention now for a few moments to the question of occultism itself. In our universities, the branch of science engaged in research into extrasensory phenomena is called parapsychology.

Over the last four decades Chairs of Parapsychology have been founded at various universities throughout the world. The first and most well-known of these is the Chair of Research into extrasensory phenomena, such as telepathy, clairvoyance and precognition or extrasensory perception (ESP), under Professor Rhine at Duke University in America. This was founded in 1934. At about the same time Professor Tenhaeff started his institute at the University of Utrecht in Holland, which was later raised to the level of a professorial chair in 1953. In 1954, Professor Bender began a similar work at Freiburg University, and in 1960 the Russians entered into the field when Professor Wassiliew received the professorship of psychical telepathy at the University of Leningrad. Ever practical, the Russians commissioned him to do research into the possibility of extrasensory influence over a distance. 1964 saw the founding of a similar parapsychological laboratory at the University of Santiago in Chile under Professor Onetto's direction.

As Christians, what are we to make of this new science? The answer to simple. Anyone who orientates himself according to Christ and accepts the Bible's view of the world, will find it almost impossible to become a parapsychologist. Every parapsychologist I know is by the nature of his work forced to take part in seances, and to experiment with spiritistic mediums, whereas the Bible explicitly forbids such a practice. In doing so the scientist brings himself into contact with the demonic (Lev. 20:27). One must remember that even scientific research has borders beyond which it should not be tempted to reach. Einstein himself recognized this fact. Shortly before his death it is said that he destroyed a mathematical formula he had discovered which would have caused the world more harm than even the hydrogen bomb.

Counselling has no part with the new science of parapsychology, unless, and it does happen, a worker in that field is convicted of his sin and his debt to Christ, and turns to the counsellor for help.

Counselling deals mainly with the more common forms of occultism as they effect the burdened and subjected person. There is time to give only a brief outline of these forms.

Occultism is divided into sometimes two and sometimes four different departments. In the fourfold division, the easiest to understand, the divisions are as follows: superstition; fortune-telling; magic; spiritism.

To take but one of these, superstition, one can find literally thousands of types of superstition in the world. Its devastating effect can be seen in the witch hunting of the Middle Ages. If an old woman had a bent or crooked nose, this was enough to mark her out as a witch and cause her to be burned. But we deceive ourselves if we think that with the enlightenment of science we have risen above such horrors as this.

The following is a true story involving a farm in North Germany. The farmer's son married a pretty girl of whom his mother was jealous. Several months after the wedding a number of the cows on the farm died. The farmer's wife began to accuse the young girl saying that she had brought bad luck on the stables. "She must be a witch," she told her husband and son. As a result of her accusations the poor girl was frequently beaten and locked up in a darkened room. She was left there without food for days. Finally, however, the process of torture was discovered and the neighbors informed the police. As a result the family was taken to court.

One could give thousands of examples illustrating the type and the effects of these four forms of occultism, but space forbids. If anyone wishes to pursue the subject further, I have dealt more fully with the different areas of occultism in my books 'The Devil's Alphabet', 'Between Christ and Satan', etc.

Those who divide occultism up into two areas base their division on the two forms of energy involved. In occultism one can differentiate between a 'causa recipiens' and a 'causa movens'. What are these? Causa recipien is the ability to use extrasensory powers to uncover the secrets of the past, present and future. This ability is called the 'psi-gamma' effect, from the Greek word 'gignoskein', meaning 'to know'. In America the phenomenon is known as ESP.

Causa movens on the other hand is the ability to influence people and objects through extrasensory forces, the so-called 'psi-kappa' effect, from the Greek word 'kinein', meaning 'to move'. In America this is called psycho-kinesis. In Europe the term telekinesis is preferred.

Every form of extrasensory perception therefore belongs to the causa recipiens side of occultism and every form of extrasensory influence to the causa movens side.

It is impossible to go into all the different areas covered by occultism, but mention should be made of at least one guise under which it often appears, that is the religious guise. In England this is manifested in the numerous spiritualistic churches and healers who claim to be working in the name of God, yet who in fact further the work of Satan. The Bible itself often suffers the abuse of being used and quoted in magic spells and formulae. And many a person is deceived by these religious accessories. The effects of white magic are just as bad as those of black magic, and a common effect indicates a common cause.

VI.   *The Effects of Occult Practices.*

From the point of view of both counselling and treating people medically, it is important to know the actual effects produced by occult involvement. Over many years now I have been able to build up the following picture of the problem. The effects of occultism on a person generally manifest themselves in five different areas.

A.   First of all the person's faith as a Christian is effected. Occultly subjected people find it all but impossible to exercise faith. They find it difficult to obtain a living relationship with Christ and as a result often fall victims to extreme sects and heresies. Those suffering in this way are plagued with doubts, find it impossible to concentrate either when reading the Bible or when praying, and they are all too often immune to the working of the Holy Spirit.

B.   Next, I have found that the person's character can be greatly changed. Occult subjection often manifests itself in the form of a violent temper, miserliness, a domineering spirit, hardness, unsociableness and so on. It can cause people to lose their self restraint, and one finds that many so-called compulsory criminals suffer from this form of occult oppression. In the same way notorious fire-raisers, alcoholics and perverts are often people who have had occult contacts in the past.

C. Next it reveals itself through the presence of mental or psychical illnesses. It often causes a person to suffer from depressions, thoughts of suicide and neuroses, although, let it be emphasized, these things in themselves do not prove the presence of the demonic.

D. A fourth effect is to be seen in a change in the mental health or state of the person concerned. Mediumistic psychoses are, at least in their symptoms, very similar to genuine psychoses, and yet different characteristics can be observed. Normally, however, because of the inability of the average psychiatrist to differentiate between medical and mediumistic psychoses, those suffering from the latter complaint often end up in psychiatric hospitals, whereas in reality only the Christian counsellor can help.

E. The last effect, and the most destructive, is what one can call hereditable mediumism. Involvement in magical practices and sorcery can effect one's children to the third and fourth generations. It is a case of the literal fulfilment of the second commandment, "visiting the iniquity of the fathers upon the children to the third and the fourth generation of those who hate me." Mediumistic subjection often appears in people's lives without any apparent cause, and it is not until later that the person concerned discovers that his depressions or hatred of God, and so on, is the result of either his grandparents' or great-grandparents' involvement in occultism. When I pointed this out to Professor Siebeck of Heidelberg University, he agreed that this is often true. As I have already intimated, I have seen this demonstrated hundreds of times over the last 30 to 40 years.

It is high time that Christian medical doctors took into account the effects that occultism can have on their patients, for only in this way will they be able to equip themselves with the tools necessary to help all those suffering from mental and psychical diseases. One cannot expect this of non-Christians in the medical profession, for to such the Bible is a completely alien book. And anyway, they are not under the same obligation as Christians to help the occultly oppressed.

VII. *Our Commission.*

This brings us almost to an end of our discussion on the effects of occultism. There is much more that could be said, but two important points must suffice.

A. Firstly, it is our duty, particularly as Christians, to come to grips and to study this neglected area of psycho-hygiene. The flood of mental diseases is growing every day. Hundreds of thousands of people are suffering oppression either directly or indirectly as a result of occult influences. The tools of medicine and psychology are inadequate for the task of dealing with this problem. Rationalism has blocked the door to a true understanding of the nature of the effect that the demonic can have upon people.

B. Secondly, we must accept the solution which the Bible offers with regards to the question of occultism. Parapsychological phenomena are often mentioned in the pages of the Old and New Testaments under the headings of divination, fortune-telling, magic, necromancy, spiritism, astrology, augury and the like. Quoting Deuteronomy 18, verses 10 to 12 just as one example, we read: "There shall not be found among you any one who burns his son or daughter as an offering, or any one who practices divination, a soothsayer, or an augur, or a sorcerer, or a charmer, or a medium, or a wizard, or a necromancer. For whoever does these things is an abomination to the Lord; and because of these abominable practices the Lord your God is driving them out before you."

In the Old Testament, sorcery was punishable by death. It was in fact considered to be a form of blasphemy. Yet the Bible does not leave the matter there. Under the New Covenant we find that Christ has made an end to the powers of darkness through His death on the cross. In 1 John 3:8 we read, "The reason the Son of God appeared was to destroy the works of the devil." And Paul confirms this in Colossians 2:15, "Christ has disarmed the principalities and powers and made a public example of them, triumphing over them in the cross." Christ has brought all the verminous powers of darkness into the light, and has trampled the head of the ancient serpent under his feet. The message of Christians today, therefore, is one of victory. The thing that concerns us is not the power of occultism but rather the power and authority of the One who overcame all the forces of evil at Calvary.

Occultism is not a hobby in which people may dabble. It is rather a problem and task which faces every minister and counsellor of Christ. It is the duty of the disciples of the Lord Jesus to give aid to those who have fallen prey to, and become ensnared by, the powers of darkness, whether through ignorance, through curiosity, or with a knowledge of the consequences involved. The only help and deliverance available is that which comes through Christ. Without him we would not be able to stand against the forces which occultism conceals. It is with gratitude therefore that we can conclude with the words of Paul the apostle on our lips:

"Death is swallowed up in victory;

O death where is your victory?

O grave where is your sting?

Thanks be to God who gives us the victory through our Lord Jesus Christ!"

Chapter 5

MIRACLES OF HEALING TODAY —
THEIR DIVINE, SUGGESTIVE OR DEMONIC CHARACTER

(An address given at the Theological Department of Waterloo University, Canada)

Summary

Introduction: Twentieth Century Healing Movements
  I.   Divine Healing.
       A.   The Charismatic Gift — 1 Corinthians 12:9
       B.   Laying on of Hands — James 5:14
       C.   Relying On God's Promises — 1 Peter 3:12
  II. Healing on the Human Level
       A.   Suggestion
       B.   Religious Suggestion
       C.   Autogenic Training
       D.   Mental Suggestion
       E.   Hypnosis
       F.   Neutral Magnetism
  III. Demonic Healing
       A.   Black and White Magic
       B.   Spiritism and Spiritualism
       C.   Fetishes, Religious and Profane
       D.   Psychometry.
       E.   Occult Suggestion; Occult Hypnosis; Occult Mental Suggestion; Occult Magnetism.

Resumé: The Gift of Discernment; Obedience; The Real Issue.

MIRACLES OF HEALING TODAY —
THEIR DIVINE, SUGGESTIVE OR DEMONIC CHARACTER.

Introduction:

There are a number of well-known healing movements and places of pilgrimage in the world today. One of the most famous of these is Lourdes, in France. Every miracle which is claimed to take place there is investigated by a group of doctors. Another place of pilgrimage is Fatima in Portugal, and another, Maria Einsiedel in Switzerland.

One of the most famous, or perhaps infamous, faith healers of this century was Padre Pio in Italy. He bore the marks (stigmata) of the cross on his hands, and each Friday these wounds would bleed. It was said that when he celebrated the Eucharist, the wafer would float from the plate to his mouth. Let me at once add, to avoid any misunderstanding, that stigmata are not a sign that God is at work. Stigmata can be produced unconsciously through autosuggestion. Neither can the phenomenon of the Host be considered as a miracle. It rather reminds me of spiritistic telekinesis. George Roux is another well-known healer from France. He is a retired post office official who claims to be Christ. The most well-known spiritual healer in England is Harry Edwards. This man is the president of a spiritistic healing movement with about 2,000 members.

One of the most successful healers in the United

States was Edgar Cayce, the so-called 'sleeping prophet'. He, too, is a spiritualistic healer like Harry Edwards, spiritualism being the religious form of spiritism.

At the moment we can only mention the different kinds of healing movements. There is no space to describe them fully.

In Pentecostal circles the name of the late William Branham is often mentioned in connection with healing. Other healers associated with Pentecostalism are T. L. Osborne, Tommy Hicks, and A. A. Allan who died under mysterious circumstances, all of whom have been hailed for their healing gifts. In this connection one must also mention Oral Roberts, who has many followers in both the United States and Latin America.

Within the present-day charismatic movement the name of Kathryn Kuhlman is also mentioned quite often. I have read both her books and have personally visited her healing meetings. This list, however, is far from complete. One could almost fill a book with the names of all the people alive today who claim to have powers of healing. One of the most powerful healers I have come across was a teacher on the island of Timor in Indonesia. Unfortunately, as a result of spiritual pride, God took away his gift.

I.   *Divine Healing.*

As a good deal of confusion exists in the field of healing, I will endeavour to give you a brief summary of the problems involved. The problem is, however, almost too large to deal with satisfactorily in the time I have available.

Before anyone begins to talk about healing,

there is a far more important biblical theme one must mention first. The spiritual welfare of a person's soul is much more important than the healing of his body. The conversion and rebirth of a man through the working of the Holy Spirit has priority over the healing of disease. Sickness or infirmity cannot keep a person out of the Kingdom of Heaven, but without the forgiveness of sins and the experience of rebirth we shall not even see the Kingdom of God.

It is important for us not to distort the problem of healing. God has given us the ability to think and reason in order that we use it. It is obviously not wrong to ask the Lord to heal us, but it is also not wrong to turn to a doctor for help. The help of a trained doctor is itself a blessing from God.

Healing should also never be sensation-alized. It should merely act as a signpost to point us to the Giver of all good gifts, our Heavenly Father. With the Scriptures in mind we can mention three forms which healing unassociated with medicine can take:

A. The charismatic gift is mentioned in 1 Corinthians 12:9. The New Testament mentions a total of twenty different gifts of the Holy Spirit in the following passages: Romans 12:6-8, 1 Corinthians 12:7-11, 28, 29. Ephesians 4:11. These gifts were all present in the primitive Church in Jerusalem.

In the history of the Church throughout the ages, however, there have been periods of drought in which these spiritual gifts have been lost sight of. Yet there have always been individual Christians who have had the courage to acknowledge their existence and use them, as, for example, Augustine, Hieronymus, Francis of Assisi, and Bernhard of Clairvaux. Miracles of healing have in fact been associated with almost every man of God. In the present century the gift of speaking in tongues has been emphasized in a number of circles, but not all so-called charismatic movements have a genuine charismatic character.

Having tried to clear the ground a little, let me say before we go on, that I am a firm believer in the gifts of the Holy Spirit. Yet the Giver of this spiritual equipment is far more important than the gifts. We must all guard against prejudice when dealing with such spiritual problems as these. Even as we rely upon God's Son for our understanding of the Father, so we will remain sound in doctrine if we gain our understanding and knowledge of the Person of the Holy Spirit through Jesus as well.

In Acts 1:8 he said, "You will receive power when the Holy Spirit comes upon you, and you shall be my witnesses." Our task therefore is to be witnesses to the Lord Jesus Christ through the power of the Holy Spirit.

Having said what I feel is very necessary to remember concerning this problem, I will now mention one example where a person was healed through her faith in Christ.

A young married couple visited a Christian worker who is a friend of mine. The young woman had a brain tumor. The doctor had told the husband, but not the woman herself, that she was incurable and would finally end up like a vegetable. The young couple were members of my friend's congregation. In his presence they both made an open confession of their sins. The minister then prayed with them and called on the Lord to heal the wife. Almost immediately the women said that she felt as if there had been a release of tension within her head. A few weeks later, when she went to the brain specialist for another check up, it was discovered that the tumor had completely disappeared. The Lord Jesus had shown his power in this young couple's life.

B.   It is rare today to find someone with a genuine gift of healing. On the other hand, the simple custom of prayer with the laying on of hands is practiced by many missionaries and evangelists on the basis of Scripture verses James 5:14, and Mark 16:17, 18. There are thousands of examples illustrating how even in the present age the Lord Jesus honors the prayers of his children under the laying on of hands. Sometimes this practice is accompanied with the anointing of the sick person with oil, again, according to the Scriptures.

However, we must not forget that it is sometimes right to refuse to lay hands on someone, especially when the person concerned is not ready to follow their Lord. Unhappily there are many cases, too, which illustrate how dangerous the laying on of hands can be when administered by occultly oppressed Christian workers.

C. Among Christians there are also a number of cases of healing where God has, in his grace, answered the simple prayers of his people. Without any special gift of healing, without the laying on of hands or anointing with oil, God can step in and answer the cries of his children. The promises of the Bible lie before us to be claimed by faith, yet this does not mean that we can ever compel God to act in a certain way. God is not our handmaid, who comes and goes at every bid and call. Our prayers and desires have to be subjected to His will.

It is our duty to encourage every believer in Christ to daily draw upon the promises God has made in his Word. Think, for example, of Jeremiah 33:3. The children of God have direct access to the Father's throne. They have a 'hot line' which they will never find engaged. At every second of the day we can reach the ear and heart of God, no matter how feeble our cry.

II. *Healing on the Human Level.*

Because of the time factor we can do little more than give a list of the areas involved. The types of healing we want to deal with in this section are on the whole not dangerous, but some of them, on account of their occult parallels, may sometimes fall within the realm of the demonic.

A. Even a simple suggestion can trigger off an improvement in one's physical health. A kind word from the family doctor can cheer the patient up and strengthen his belief that he is going to get better. And it is not only the doctor who can do this. Close relatives can also be a source of great strength to the ailing person.

B. Suggestion can also make its appearance on the religious level, particularly among groups of primitive Christians. For example:

I once visited the meetings of a certain faith healer. After he had finished preaching he addressed himself to those in the meeting who were sick or ill. I was able to watch as he then laid hands on a young man in a wheel chair and said, "In the name of the Lord Jesus you are healed. Stand up!" The paralyzed man, using all his strength, raised himself up on the arms of the wheel chair and stood trembling on both legs. The faith healer cried at him, "Come on now, take a few steps." The man started to force himself to walk forward a little, but then collapsed. Being put back into his wheel chair he was then wheeled out of the hall. Next morning the young man came to see me for counselling. "The paralysis is worse than ever now," he told me, and went on, "How can this faith healer play about so lightly with the name of Jesus?" A few days later a member of the local Pentecostal group went to see the young man, and while he was talking to him he said, "You would have been healed now if you had really believed."

One could quote hundreds of examples like this, but the faith that is talked of in James 5:14 is not just the faith of the sick man, it includes the faith of the elders as well.

Religious suggestion is not a form of divine healing. The prime mover in a genuine case of biblical healing is the living God, whereas in a case of religious suggestion the impulse comes from a religiously orientated man. Biblical healings are deep and lasting in their effects. Religious suggestion is not. It is a sign of the terrible spiritual chaos of our times that religious suggestion is so often labelled as 'divine healing' by Christians who should know better.

C.   Autogenic training originated in the Far East, and is often associated with meditation. The person chiefly responsible for its introduction into Europe is Professor Schultz of Berlin. Autogenic training is based on an idea common to a number of different philosophies. One can think of the book by Norman Vincent Peale entitled *The Power of Positive Thinking*. Then there is the Christian Science movement whose representatives talk of the 'healing idea'. In the same way, in the first stage of Yoga one finds exercises in concentration and meditation designed to enable the spirit to gain mastery over the body. All these systems are founded upon the same idea, or start at the same point, namely: through self-control man must learn to master himself.

Even though this starting point is understandable from the human point of view, I nevertheless strongly reject its application in the spiritual or religious realm. From the Christian point of view these efforts to obtain healing are nothing more than an attempt at salvation by works.

One episode I remember is of interest in connection with the area we have just been talking about. A patient of Professor Schultz told me in March 1972 that Professor Schultz's female assistant had once used a pendulum during one of the sessions he had had with her. We have here a fusion between autogenic training and occult practices, but the fault is that of Professor Schultz's assistant rather than the professor himself.

D.   I have come across mental suggestion not only in the field of telepathy but also within Christian Science and other movements.

As an example of this I can mention, how two French doctors succeeded in influencing a 16-year-old girl, one over a distance of 8 km, and the other over a distance of 16 km. One could also think of this as a type of hypnosis. In the world of occultism mental suggestion occurs in a much stronger form than it does on the human level.

E.   Hypnotism is a highly controversial subject. The famous psychologist, Dr. Paul Tournier of Geneva in Switzerland rejects its use entirely. He argues that hypnotism illegally interferes with the subconscious mind and the soul of man. On the other hand I have met missionaries who have regarded hypnotism as a means of obtaining healing.

I will quote an example concerning the Head Doctor of the Cruz Blanca Sanatorium, Esquil, Argentina.

One of the doctor's patients was a woman suffering from a pronounced complex. She was convinced that her house was full of spiders, in spite of the fact that there were none there at all. Hypnotizing her, the doctor told her that when she regained consciousness the spiders would be gone. The experiment was successful. Yet from that time onwards the woman began to develop a strong alcoholic addiction, something she had never suffered from before. The doctor told me that because this transference had taken place, he now had reservations about using hypnotism in his practice.

A similar example to this was told me in the Swiss canton of Berne while I was counselling a person there.

A Christian woman was hypnotized by a doctor while she was suffering from a gall-stone colic. The hypnosis was surprisingly successful and the almost unbearable pain disappeared within minutes. Afterwards, however, the woman began to suffer from terrible outbursts of rage. For example, she would sometimes throw the crockery or the glasses at the wall in fury, a thing she had never done or felt inclined to do before. In this case the hypnosis had triggered off a lack of self-control, and the many similar examples I have come across in my work have led me too to reject the use of hypnosis as a means of therapy. But each person is free to form his own conclusions.

F. Natural magnetism. A number of well-known missionaries in Europe are convinced that while about 10% of all healing magnetism is neutral or safe, the other 90% is occultly based. In my own counselling experience I have come across only a very few cases of natural magnetism which has no connection with occultism. And when it is neutral, it is also very weak. Strong forms of magnetism are only found in the demonic area. A man who practiced healing magnetism once came to me to be counselled. He told me, "Natural magnetism enables a person to treat only one or two patients each day. Whoever has powers of healing magnetism to treat more than two people a day is plugged in to the underworld."

There are many people, particularly in the Far East, who are able to cure or to help people suffering from headaches, rheumatism, and arthritis by making stroking movements over them with their hands, but whenever I have come across a person who possesses this gift, I have always found that either his parents, grandparents or great-grandparents have dabbled in magic or spiritism. For this reason, even in the case of natural magnetism I am not altogether happy with its use.

III. *Demonic Healing.*

The New Testament itself bears clear testimony to the existence of demonic forms of healing: Matthew 24:24, Mark 13:22, 2 Thessalonians 2:8, 9, Revelation 13:13; 16:14.

Demonic healings can be divided into two different types, the profane form and the religious form. What this means is that the devil has learned to play on everyone's piano! The godless he ensnares through profane miracles of healings not connected with Christianity at all, while Christians are seduced by miracles dressed in a religious guise. There is a terrible error being propagated in the world today whereby demonic healings, because of the Christian facade behind which they take place, are being claimed as charismatic miracles. One minister wrote me a furious letter claiming that his ability to use a pendulum was a gift from God, and as such had to be used for the benefit of mankind. It was unthinkable for him to believe that mediumistic healings are basically occult and not charismatic in character.

Let me quote an example to help illustrate the problem.

A woman who was a nominal Christian allowed her child whose body was covered with a skin infection to be treated by a magical charmer. A spell was said over the child three times in the name of the Trinity. The use of the names of the Father, the Son and the Holy Spirit was designed to give people the impression that the treatment was biblical, which it most certainly was not. The little girl, however, was healed. But that is not the end of the story. Afterwards the mother started to have difficulty in praying and reading her Bible. When she listened to sermons in the church her mind seemed unable to concentrate. Her daughter, too, began to suffer from depressions as she grew up, and the situation was sometimes so bad that both mother and daughter thought of committing suicide. Finally, on attending a mission meeting they both stayed behind to talk to the evangelist. Making a complete and open confession of their sins, they handed their lives over to Christ, and received the forgiveness which he alone can offer. A few days later the daughter's old eczema returned. This time two Christian brothers prayed for her healing, and God answered their prayers. She was healed for good.

The example can be summarized briefly in the following way: illness - a magical cure - the developments of emotional disturbances - genuine conversion - recurrence of the old illness. Let us look further into the pattern which has emerged.

The human mind or soul can psychologically be split into seven different levels (see diagram), the lowest level being the organic realm. It is here that all organic illnesses take place. The next level is that of the organic unconsciousness, the psycho-physical transfer-station. Here organic impulses are transformed into physical reactions, and vice versa. The third level is the collective subconsciousness where traces of mankind's history are stored. Next comes the family subconsciousness, and then the individual subconsciousness where traces of one's childhood's experiences are stored. The sixth level is that of consciousness itself, the level of conscious experience and action. And lastly we have the superconsciousness, the realm of genius, the artist's vision, and intuition. This house of seven stories has an elevator running from top to bottom. Organic illness at the lowest level can give rise to psychical reactions which in turn can affect the subconscious and the conscious. In the same way mental resolutions or emotional experiences can trigger off downward impulses which are finally transformed into organic reactions. But to save boring you with a lot of psychological argument, let me quote some more examples which illustrate the principle quite clearly.

Psychoporganic Relationships.

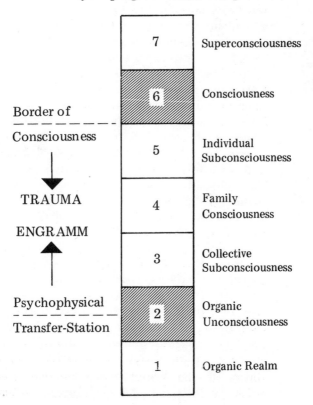

7	Superconsciousness
6	Consciousness
5	Individual Subconsciousness
4	Family Consciousness
3	Collective Subconsciousness
2	Organic Unconsciousness
1	Organic Realm

Border of
Consciousness

↓

TRAUMA

ENGRAMM

↑

Psychophysical
Transfer-Station

In a disease of the liver, for example icterus, initially the illness is confined to the lowest level, i.e. the organic realm. As time goes on, however, impulses are transferred from stage to stage until the patient begins to feel moody, irritable, and perhaps even suffer from depressions. And so we see that the organic illness has concomitant phenomena associated with it.

To illustrate the reverse procedure let me refer to one of my own experiences. I once met a student who was a master of Yoga. He was able, for example, to produce stigmata on his own hands merely by auto-suggestion. How did he do this? He would begin to concentrate on the palm of one of his hands. Gradually the palm would turn red as the circulation increased. Then the blood would start to come through the pores of the skin, and so the stigma was produced. It was a case of transference from the higher to the lower levels. The mental concentration caused a change to take place in the organic realm.

When a transference takes place from the upper levels to the lower levels, in psychological terminology a 'trauma' is said to have taken place. This word is actually a Greek word, meaning 'injury'. On the other hand a transfer upwards from the lower levels is called an 'engramm', coming from the Greek word 'engrapho', meaning to 'engrave'. Although a great deal of research has been done in Germany into the nature of traumas, the whole science of psychotherapy being based upon this research, little attention has been paid to the reverse procedure of engramms. In fact the work of one pioneer in this field, Professor Weizaecker, has been almost completely ignored.

For ourselves, what we can learn from this psychological introduction is that demonic healing always results in an engramm taking place, i.e. a transference from the lower to the upper levels. The original organic illness is shifted higher into the psychical realm, with the result that while the physical illness disappears, new disorders appear in the mental and emotional life of the person concerned, disorders which are in fact far more difficult to treat and cure. Magical healings are therefore not really healings at all, but merely transferences from the organic to the physical level.

So far so good, but in counselling work one discovers that the problem is even more involved than what we have just mentioned.

Firstly, one does not realize the force with which these transfers are accompanied.

Secondly, the transfers cannot be reversed, the wheel cannot be turned back, except through the power of Christ.

And thirdly, these magical transfers act as a blockage to a person's spiritual life.

Because of this, a person who has experienced a transference of this nature is in need of authoritative Christian counselling, and experience shows that only those who are ready and willing to hand their lives over to Christ completely, can experience deliverance.

The damage caused through magical healing is immense, and since this damage occurs mainly in the spiritual lives of the people who are healed, one is forced to describe the power behind it as demonic. This can be confirmed by the following example.

A woman who was seriously ill lay in hospital suffering from shingles and leg ulcers. Her condition was so critical that the doctor ordered a nurse to remain by her bedside for the whole night. It was expected that she would die. Sitting next to her, the night nurse heard the patient begin to whisper, "Nurse, you can help me. Nurse, you can help me." The nurse felt afraid, but the woman kept on, "Nurse, you can help me." In the end the nurse asked the sick woman, "What do you want me to do? How can I help you?" The woman began to get excited and said to the nurse, "Put your hand on my legs and make the sign of the cross over them three times, then say the name of the Trinity and repeat the verse I will tell you." The night nurse was now even more frightened, but at that moment the doctor walked by the ward. Asking him what she ought to do, the doctor replied, "Oh, do what she asks you. It might even help her. There's no hope for her from the medical point of view." She returned to the bed. Immediately the patient began to encourage her again to begin the charming process. Finally the nurse did what she asked, and made the sign of the cross three times over her body, murmuring the names of the Trinity and the spell she had been told. The patient relaxed. She could rest. The nurse, however, was suddenly overwhelmed by a tremendous agitation and fear.

In the days that followed the medical staff was astonished. The open ulcers on the woman's legs closed up almost at once, and within five days all symptoms of her illness had completely disappeared. The doctor who knew about the charming kept the incident to himself.

Today, six years have passed since the woman was healed, but the nurse who attended her has never been at peace since. She cannot pray. She cannot listen to the gospel without feeling a sense of disgust. She often feels as if she is in a daze, that she cannot concentrate properly, and she now suffers from a number of emotional disturbances. Because of her condition she came to see me in order to get some help through counselling. In her own mind she traces every one of the psychical and emotional disturbances back to the night during which she sat with the woman. Without realizing it she had used white magic in order to heal the woman's complaint.

Having laid a foundation to enable us to understand the problem more easily, we can now make a list of the most frequest forms of demonic healing.

A.   Black magic is the most widespread profane form of demonic healing in the world. People who use black magic either promise or subscribe the soul of the person who is ill to the devil as payment for the healing they receive. White magic, the religious form of black magic, functions in a similar way. The two examples we have quoted already in this section illustrate this fact. In white magic the name of God and Bible verses are often misused. The false prophet who is yet to come will be a master in this art. One of the signs of the terrible confusion in the world today is the fact that many ministers and pastors look on white magic as a scriptural idea. It is a fulfilment of the words of Paul in 2 Corinthians 11:14, "Satan disguises himself as an angel of light."

B. Spiritistic healing also has its religious form, namely spiritualistic healing. Both Harry Edwards and Edgar Cayce are examples of men who practice in this field. Harry Edwards claims in fact that more than a hundred Anglican ministers have come to him for help. This is a sign of how good the religious disguise can be. Edwards goes on to say that he is only able to heal when his good spirits are present, a claim which many faith healers have made in recent years.

C. Where fetishes are involved, before healing can take place an object with magical powers is first of all required. In Africa and East Asia the people prefer to use the claws of a wild cat or the teeth of a beast of prey as fetishes. These objects become sources of healing power. The principle at work goes back thousands of years, the people believing for example that if they possess the claws of an animal, they possess the animal's strength as well.

It is sad to say, but religious fetishes have also existed since time immemorial. The bronze snake which Moses lifted up in the wilderness (Numbers 21) later became a snare to the children of Israel, a symbol of sorcery (2 Kings 18:4). The handkerchiefs of the apostle (Acts 19:12), a sign of the childlike faith of the early Church, later became a superstitious symbol. The relics kept by many churches are also often nothing more than religious fetishes. How many priests can one think of that have recommended people to carry some religious medallion which has been specially blessed.

D.   The term psychometry is unfortunately used in different ways in the United States and England. Lately it has become the fashion to describe certain psychological tests by this word. At the same time, however, it is used to describe an occult and mediumistic ability which a number of people possess. A person who practices psychometry will ask his patient for some object which he will use to diagnose the disease and decide its therapy. The object may be anything from a handerchief to a pair of socks, or from a shirt to some fingernail cuttings. One psychometrist I know of in France even uses the saliva of his patients. In this way the psychometrist can use his mediumistic intuition to discover the actual nature of the disease which he then endeavors to cure using occultly based mental suggestion. Even graphology, the study of handwriting, can be used as a form of psychometry. An example: I know an occult psychometrist in St. Gallen in Switzerland who, when patients write to him for help will concentrate on the handwriting of the letters he receives. By so doing he can determine the nature of the patient's illness which he then tries to heal by concentrating on the patient himself. A person with a genuine psychometric ability can in fact obtain almost anything he wants to know from the handwriting of a patient. The phenomenon is in fact closely related to that of clairvoyance.

It was most revealing for me to discover that a well-known faith healer in North America regarded a female psychometrist in New York as someone richly blessed by God because of her ability. I heard the faith healer say this with my own ears.

E.   Religious suggestion, hypnosis, mental suggestions and magnetism have already been mentioned under the heading 'Healing on the Human Level'. Each of these, however, has its occult counterpart. Regrettably only a small percentage of these phenomena are neutral in character. The demonic form is practiced far more fre-

quently. The healing ability of the
psychometrist in the example we have just
mentioned is closely associated with occult
mental suggestion. I can quote an example
of occult hypnosis to help us understand
the problem more clearly. It comes from a
Baptist minister in the United States who
gave me permission to publish the account.

In the autumn of 1971 I spoke at one
of the services at his church. Afterwards,
while I was having lunch with him, the
minister told me the story of his
16-year-old son. When he had been at college, the son had taken part in one of the
school's entertainment evenings. The high-
light of the evening came when a hypnotist
invited 25 of the students to come up onto
the stage and them hypnotized them. He
suggested to them that they were all taking
part in a horse race. With that the students
started moving about on their chairs as if
they were riding horses. When the act
ended, the hypnotist told the students to
come back out of their hypnotic states.
The minister's son, however, remained in a
trance. The college president was extremely
worried. In the end they were forced to call
the hospital, and the boy was taken away
in an ambulance. The doctors attempted
again to bring him out of his hypnotic
state, but with no success. It was only after
five days had passed that his father was
finally notified as to what had happened.
Immediately he had his son transferred to

his own home. Together with his wife and some friends they began to pray for the boy. Yet even then the hypnotic effect was not broken. In the end, when a few more days had elapsed, the father felt constrained to command his son in the name of Jesus. To his amazement, his son responded at once. The hypnotic effect was broken.

I could quote many examples like this involving so-called harmless hypnotists. People must be warned of the dangers involved in allowing their children to take part in what they think are only harmless hypnotic games.

The unfortunate thing is that occult hypnosis is often used as a means of obtaining healing. The apparent success of the hypnosis, however, is accompanied without fail with all sorts of mental and emotional disturbances. As the previous example shows, even qualified doctors are unable to undo the damage done by occult forms of hypnosis. The problem is not a medical one, but rather a religious one. The encouraging thing in all this is, however, that the name of Jesus shines through as being stronger than all the wiles and powers of the devil.

Resumé.

I. In spiritual matters any shift of emphasis is dangerous. Salvation is always more important than healing. The forgiveness of a person's sins is greater than physical health.

II. The confusion in the minds of people today is so great that not only religious suggestion but even spiritualism and white magic are regarded by some to be sources of divine healing.

III. There are many so-called faith healers and spiritistic healers who use the name of Jesus in their work, and yet who one day will be rejected by the Lord himself (Matthew 7:22).

IV. There are cases of healing today which have an appearance of being divinely inspired and yet which in reality are the devil's own work.

V. These demonic healings are only a ruse whereby Satan, in exchange for organic help, ruins a person's soul.

VI. Demonic healings are not true forms of healing but merely represent a shift of the problem from the organic to the psychical realm. The person who is healed is the victim of a terrible confidence trick.

VII. The effects of these occult forms of healing can often be seen for years in the spiritual and mental life of the victim.

VIII. If a person is not delivered from these effects by Jesus Christ, Satan will demand that the price be paid even after death.

IX. Through Christ, however, this spiritual confidence trick can be reversed. The Son of God paid the price for us all on the cross.

X. In all the chaos surrounding divine healing, Christians need the gift of discernment more than anything else

XI. As the apostle Paul writes in 1 Corinthians 14:1,

we should desire the higher gifts, not to boast, but for the edification of others.

XII. There is in the twentieth century a genuine unfolding of the gifts of the Holy Spirit among believers, those who have really been born of the Spirit of God.

XIII. The Holy Spirit has not gone out of business merely because he does not fit into the concepts of a number of modern theologians.

XIV. We have the same God today, the same Saviour, the self same Holy Spirit and the same promises as the early Church in Jerusalem. His Glory belongs to us as well as them (John 17:22).

XV. The Giver of the gifts is always more important than the gifts themselves, as is our obedience to him.

XVI. Healing is therefore not the burning issue in our lives. The most important factor is our relationship with the Holy Triune God:

the Father of mercies,

the crucified, risen and returning Lord, and the Holy Spirit who intercedes for us with groans which cannot be uttered (Romans 8:26).

Chapter 6

DEMON POSSESSION AND THE
WAY OF DELIVERANCE.

(Address given at the Theological Department of the University of Buenos Aires, Argentina)

Summary

   I.   Medicine and Modern Theology.
  II.   Eight Marks of Demon Possession: The Case of the Possessed Gadarene.
 III.   The Case of the Possessed Philippino Student.
 IV.   The Way of Deliverance
      A.   Jesus the Only Saviour
      B.   The Counsellor's Spiritual Armour
      C.   Medically Ill or Occultly Oppressed?
      D.   Destruction of Fetishes, Idols and Occult Books
      E.   Breaking Mediumistic Contacts
      F.   Confession
      G.   Forgiveness
      H.   Renunciation
      I.   Absolution
      J.   Loosing
      K.   Prayer Groups
      L.   Praying and Fasting
      M.   The Lord's Protection
      N.   Commanding in the Name of Christ

O. Means of Grace
P. The Armour of God
Q. Realizing the Victory.
R. The Return of Evil Spirits

DEMON POSSESSION AND THE
WAY OF DELIVERANCE.

The New Testament often talks about demon possessed people being healed by the power of Christ. Today, however, in the medical and theological worlds, there are very few who believe in the existence of demon possession. Everything is explained away in terms of psychical abnormalities. We have no choice, therefore, but to begin our discussion by considering this attitude adopted by so many people in the world today.

I. *Medicine and Modern Theology.*

Thinking first of all of psychiatry, the study of mental and nervous disorders, like all branches of science it relies for its data on observations which can be measured and tested in the laboratory. It is therefore not good to expect any branch of science to speak with authority about the existence of either God, the devil, or demons. This is beyond their scope. Thus when the Christian worker confronts a demon possessed person out of whom foreign voices begin to speak, the only way the psychiatrist or psychologist can explain this is by resorting to the idea of schizophrenia. Whether or not this at times is the correct explanation is not our concern at the moment. We are merely trying to outline the fundamental problems in this area.

Psychotherapy is another branch of medical science which rejects the reality of possession. This particular field of research is a mere 70 years old, and is closely associated with the names of Freud, Adler and Jung. One need do no more than briefly mention what these pioneers of psychotherapy said.

A.   Freud, for example, was of the opinion that psychical abnormalities like hysteria were the effect of some sexual frustration. A human being who is sexually repressed or who lacks normal sexual expression, can become mentally unbalanced as a result of the pressures this causes. Freud was basically interested in the cause of mental abnormalities.

B.   Adler on the other hand was interested more in the patient's actual desires and drives, and their effect on his mental health. He was convinced that a hysterical person only feigns illness in order to attain his real desires. His point was that mental disorders depend not so much on an innate cause, as upon a desire for a certain effect in the person concerned. The question he always asked therefore was, what is the patient actually trying to achieve?

C.   Jung, who is perhaps the most illustrious of the depth psychologists, tried to explain everything in terms of inheritance. We are influenced, he said, by our racial past and the collective unconsciousness, and these factors as they reside in the individual's unconscious mind determine his behavior and thoughts. It is not so much we who make the decisions as our heredity.

The problem of demon possession was therefore not taken seriously by any of these three men. It was simply explained away as some form of mental blockage.

But this is not all. In spite of the opinions of men of science like these, what do modern theologians have to say on the subject?

First of all I would like to say a few words about a German theologian whose ideas have captured the minds of many people today. Professor Bultmann, in one of his books entitled *Kerygma and Myth* says these words, "The idea of Satan and demons is finished. Finished is the theory of the Virgin Birth. Finished is the question of whether Jesus of Nazareth is God's Son or not. Finished is the teaching of substitutionary atonement, the resurrection, and the ascension. Finished is the belief in the Second Coming. Finished are the miracles and answers to prayer." On reading such words as this one might well ask, "Well, what remains then of the Bible?" We have no time at the moment to answer all the problems a theology like this raises, and in fact it is not even worth the time. Jesus is either the Son of God or he is not. It is as decisive as that. Let me therefore say just one thing. Bultmann maintains that the teaching in the New Testament is derived from the mythological concepts of the old world, and that it therefore does not apply to us today. This is the basic error of all his criticism. It was in the incarnation of Christ in fact that the mythology of the old world was finally smashed. The Son of God broke into the history of mankind. The fact of the crucifixion, the disciples' testimony to the resurrection, the growth of the early Church, strike at the very heart of the myths surrounding the ancient world. A theology which denies the reality of these events can therefore be rejected, together with the arguments of the various medical and psychological sciences, when it comes to the question of demon possession and the spiritual world.

II. *Eight Marks of Demon Possession.*

In Luke 8:26-33, 38, 39 we find the story of the possessed Gadarene. If we examine the account to discover if there are any characteristics which are typical of possession, we find eight marks or symptoms which distinguish demon possession from mental and nervous diseases.

A. The first fact we are faced with is that in demon possession demons are actually resident in the person concerned. Mark describes them as evil spirits. The phenomenon is the counterpart of the indwelling of the Holy Spirit in a believer.

I have often been asked what I think evil spirits really are. Are they just demons, or are they the souls of the dead taking possession of the living, or are they something else?

The Bible does not give us the answer to these questions. We must therefore be careful when we approach the problem. The Scriptures seem to teach that the dead are not free to roam where they will, but are under God's control. It is difficult therefore to know what to make of the voices which sometimes speak out of possessed people purporting to be the spirits of their ancestors.

In France, for example, I was faced once with a possessed woman. The voices which spoke out of her claimed to be the spirits of her dead grandfather and grandmother who had both dabbled in sorcery. One explanation which commends itself to me is that if the grandmother herself had been possessed, when she died the evil spirit may have left her body and transferred itself into one of her descendents, claiming to be the grandmother's spirit. The demon would in this way be a lying spirit trying to deceive us.

B. The second sign of possession is the unusual strength exhibited by the possessed person. The Gadarene demoniac was able to break the ropes and chains which bound him. When I was in the Philippines, the frail young man I had to deal with who under normal circumstances I would easily have been able to contain, sometimes needed nine grown men to hold him down when the supernatural rage struck him.

C. The third sign is the visible conflict within the possessed person. One meets a similar phenomenon in psychiatry, where doctors talk of split personalities or disintegration. In the case of the Gadarene, on the one hand we see him coming to Jesus apparently for help, and on the other hand he suddenly reacts in fear and begs him not to torment him.

D. Next we have the phenomenon of resistance, an opposition to the things of God. "What have you to do with me," the Gadarene cried out. This resistance is exhibited by every person who is demon possessed. The student at Manila, whom I will mention later, cried out every time I addressed him in the name of Jesus, "Don't mention that name. I can't stand it."

E. The fifth sign is clairvoyance. The Gadarene knew who Jesus was immediately as he saw him, although they had never met before. He recognized too, that Jesus had the power to deliver him and to drive the demons out. I have found in counselling such people that they sometimes have the ability even to name the sins of the people present.

One possessed woman I was dealing with suddenly jumped up, seized the jacket of a minister who was also present, and screamed, "You hypocrite. Put your own life in order before you try to help others." No Christian should attempt to help a demon possessed person unless his own sins are completely forgiven.

F. The next mark of possession is the ability of the person to speak with voices not his own. A possessed woman in Southern Germany often used to speak with a man's voice during the time of her attacks. The student from Manila spoke with several voices including that of a woman. The possessed Gadarene did the same.

It is not sufficient to explain this phenomenon by describing it as a case of schizophrenia, for in many instances the voices actually use foreign languages which the victim does not even know. This is in fact one of the strongest arguments against the explanations of modern science and theology. No mentally ill or hysterical person can suddenly start speaking in a foreign language which he has never learned.

G. The seventh mark or sign that a person is demon possessed is the sudden deliverance which is possible. Our psychiatrists know full well how long and tedious the treatment for a mentally deranged person can be. Possessed people on the other hand can be delivered almost instantaneously when they come into contact with the Lord Jesus Christ.

H. The last characteristic I intend to mention is that of transference. When the Gadarene demoniac was delivered, some 2,000 pigs went berserk and rushed headlong into the sea. Events like this don't occur in medicine. I could give several examples to illustrate what I mean, but one, about a pastor in Switzerland, must suffice.

The man in question grew up in a family in which sorcery was practiced. His father was an active spiritist and magician. When however, an evangelist turned up in the village and held a mission there, the father and one of his sons who was actually demon possessed were soundly converted. Immediately after this happened the pigs in a nearby pigsty started squealing, and began to run around all over the place. After a period of five hours, during which time nothing could be done to calm them down, the farmer had to shoot them all. The converted son later entered a seminary and became a pastor. He gave me permission to publish this story.

This brings us to an end of our brief resumé of the marks of possession as exhibited by the possessed Gadarene. It may be of interest to one to realize that the Catholic Church also recognizes the reality of demon possession. In fact in the Missal they mention four signs by which one can recognize the presence of possession. These are:

1. Knowledge of a language previously unknown;
2. Knowledge of hidden or secret things;
3. Demonstration of superhuman strength;
4. An aversion to the things of God.

III. *The Case of a Possessed Philippino Student.*
Before we go on to discuss the way a person can be delivered from the power of evil spirits, I would like to mention the case of a young student I helped counsel in Manila in the Philippines.

I was on a lecture tour of the Far East when I had the opportunity of visiting the Bible School of Febias in Manila. While I was there, one of the students, who was in fact a Christian, went to see Dr. Hufstetler, the director of the school. He complained of a terrible headache and of feeling sick, and he asked Dr. Hufstetler to pray for him. While the director prayed, the student suddenly lost consciousness and began to get into a fury. It took several men to hold him down. By this time, I and a few others had been called to help deal with him. In our presence strange voices began to speak out of his mouth. One of the teachers present therefore addressed these voices, "In the name of the Lord

Jesus, tell us why you have possessed Pat," (the student's name was Pat Tolosa). "Because he did not surrender his life completely," the voices responded. "How many are you," we went on. "Fifty," they replied again.

Let me point out an important fact. I have been asked on a number of occasions whether or not believers can be demon possessed. My usual reply is, "Some theologians believe it's impossible for the Holy Spirit and demons to reside in the same body. Theoretically I agree with this, but my counselling work has shown that genuine Christians can become the victims of demon possession. The only explanation seems to me that such demon possession is a very extreme form of temptation." In Pat Tolosa's case, he had been a Christian for about a year, but the key seemed to be that although he had confessed his sins and received forgiveness and the assurance of salvation, he had not yielded his life completely to Christ. On top of this, his mother had been an active sorceress. These two facts appeared to be the factor that had allowed him to become possessed.

This should be a warning to all of us. An uncommitted life is an open door for the devil's attacks. We can have our sins forgiven, and have peace with God, but still be living a life which is not fully surrendered to Christ.

We continued to counsel the boy. "In the name of the Lord I command you to come out of him," I said. "No," they replied, "we need somebody to live in." "In the name of the Lord you have to go," I repeated. "Then we will go into the children of Dr. Hufstetler," they answered. Now it was Dr. Hufstetler's turn to speak. "You cannot enter my children. Go instead to where Jesus sends you."

We continued to command them to go, singing the hymn 'There is power in the blood of the Lamb' to give strength to our prayers. Suddenly the student began to scream. His whole body convulsed. Then he became quiet for a few moments without gaining consciousness. We prayed again, and as we did so a new voice began to speak. "How many of you are left," I asked the voice. "Forty nine," it replied. An hour had already gone by. What could we expect to happen next?

While all this had been going on, some of the Christian teachers got together and began to support us in prayer. More and more of the students joined them, until towards the end two groups were meeting simultaneously for prayer and praise. We found, too, that no single person was able to confront the demons for more than a short period at a time, the effort being too strenuous. In fact, the whole session lasted from 8 o'clock Friday morning until half past three the following Saturday morning, a total of nineteen and a half hours.

In the process of all this, one of the teachers commanded the voices, "In the name of Jesus tell us your name." "Rakrek," the voice replied. "Where do you come from?" the teacher continued. "From Manchuria," came the reply. "In the name of Jesus tell us why you have come to our school!" "You have a good school. We have come to bring in modernism and liberalism. You won't be able to stop us. They are our friends." I thought at the time how good it would have been if all the modern theologians of the world could have been present to hear these words.

When I heard that the voice had come from Manchuria, I recited a Russian Bible verse which I knew. Then came a surprise. The voice immediately began to speak in fluent Russian in spite of the fact that Pat Tolosa was acquainted with only English and his own Philippino dialect.

Again we commanded the demons to depart in the name of the Lord, and again the student shrieked and convulsed and became quiet for a short while. "How many of you are there now," we asked. "Forty eight," was the reply. We realized that quite a battle lay ahead of us. If one described all that took place it would fill a book.

As the struggle proceeded, one of the demons answered, "We have come to destroy Pat." Instantly the possessed boy tried to choke himself. He had to be forcibly restrained, sometimes by six, and sometimes by up to nine men. His strength was enormous. They went on, "Pat betrayed the communists. Therefore we are going to kill him." Of course, not everything they said was true, but their derisive laughter gave them away whenever they tried to mislead us. "In the name of Jesus tell us the truth," we would say, and with that they were no longer able to lie. The Russian demon told us that a group of communists in Manila were planning to do away with Pat. One of them, he said, was shadowing him already, waiting for a chance to kill.

When we learned this, a psychiatrist who was present notified the police. The School Board did in fact call in both a Christian psychiatrist and a Christian psychologist to assist in the struggle. Both of these men were fully convinced that the boy was possessed and not ill.

In one of the phases of the battle the demons even attacked me by name. "Why don't you leave us alone, Dr. Koch?" they asked. "Your books have done us a lot of harm in Europe, and now you come to the Philippines too." It was an encouragement to hear this, but a danger too, for pride always comes before a fall.

As the demons were being cast out we gradually became aware of the fact that they came from all over the world, which explained the different languages some of them spoke. It also became apparent how they had received their orders from Satan, orders which they had to adhere to till the end.

Suddenly one of the voices said to me, "With the strongest hypnosis of Sumatra go into a trance." Pat's eyes seemed to flash at this instance with a fiery look, but in the name of Jesus I said, "I laugh at your hypnosis. The blood of Christ protects me." The demon began to scream, "With the strongest black magic of Egypt and the most powerful black magic of Tibet I will kill you." I repeated what I had said before, "The blood of Christ protects me." This demon too was forced to leave.

Another voice claimed to come from Holland and to have originated from an occult circle there. Others cried out, and this was significant, "The Lord is coming in glory with his holy angels. Give us more time, give us more time." Every one of them was dominated by a fear of the name and the coming of the Lord.

In the end, however, Pat was wonderfully freed. After almost a day he regained consciousness when the last demon finally left. At first he began to cry and then he began to praise the Lord. It was only later when we told him, that he realized what had actually been taking place. All the teachers and students present joined together in repentance and prayer. We placed ourselves afresh under the protection of the blood of Christ, encouraging one another continually in prayer and song. It had been an overwhelming experience.

Let us just recapitulate the most important lessons of this unique counselling experience.

A. The boy had become possessed because he had not surrendered himself completely to Christ. Besides this there was a strong occult oppression on his family because of his mother's sorcery.

B. The demons were pursuing aims given to them by Satan himself.

C. The demons were able to tell us about things we did not know from all over the world.

D.   The demons all respected and feared the name of Jesus.

E.   The demons were counting on the early return of the Lord in His glory.

IV. *The Way of Deliverance.*

In the section which follows I have briefly compiled everything I can find in the New Testament regarding the question of deliverance. What has been proved in experience a thousand times over is that occult subjection and demon possession are spiritual concepts, which can only be adequately dealt with through counselling based on the Scriptures.

As we go through the following eighteen points concerning counselling the occultly oppressed, we must guard against merely thinking of them as a system, or method of approach. In the work of God on earth, there are no blueprints. Every person is an individual in the sight of God. Thus every counselling session unfolds in its own individual way. The eighteen points are only signposts to indicate the overall picture of such work. They also form only a quick sketch of the whole problem. If a person wants more information he can turn to my book 'Occult Bondage and Deliverance', or to the more scientific work 'Christian Counselling and Occultism'.

Concerning the counselling of demonically oppressed people we can mention the following points.

A.   Jesus is the only one able to free people from occult oppression. Psychiatrists, psychologists and theologians at most are only a poor substitute. Satan is a powerful enemy. He has only been defeated once: at the cross on Golgotha where the archenemy was dethroned. If an oppressed person is unwilling to come to Jesus he can hold out no hope of being delivered. A tragic example from France illustrates this only too well.

A woman went to a Christian for help. Her husband had several years previously subscribed himself to the devil with his own blood just as a joke. It was only afterwards that he realized what a bondage and liability he let himself in for. He wanted to be freed. His wife was a Christian and had prayed a great deal for him, but he was not prepared to truly follow Christ. He wanted someone to break the chain in which he had become enmeshed, but he also wanted to continue to be his own master. For this reason he has till now been unable to get free.

The apostle John said, "If the Son makes you free, you will be free indeed" (John 8:36). But it is only through the Son that we can be freed.

B.   Although we have said that Jesus is the sole source of all help, he nevertheless often makes use of a counsellor in the process. When this is the case, it is absolutely essential that the counsellor has the spiritual armor necessary for the strenuous task of dealing with the occultly oppressed. This armor we can only list briefly.

1.   If the counsellor is himself occultly subjected, he can never hope to help others in the same condition.

2.   The counsellor must be sound in faith. Modernists and extremists only do harm when they engage in this work.

3.   The counsellor must have experienced the rebirth through the working of the Holy Spirit.

4.   If possible the counsellor should have had some medical training. A knowledge of psychiatry, for example, can often be of help when endeavouring to diagnose what is really wrong.

5.   The counsellor should pray unceasingly for the gift of discernment.

6.   A counsellor should if possible have a number of years experience behind him. A young man should exercise restraint in this type of work, and call in older men to help.

7.   Christians of a nervous disposition should not attempt this type of work. Similarly enthusiastic young women should not attempt to counsel the demonically

oppressed. As Scriptures say, "Let not many of you become teachers." The dangers involved in this form of counselling can be illustrated by examples from three of my friends.

In Germany the leader of a Christian home who had studied both medicine and theology invited me to hold some meetings there. As a result of listening to my talks and the reading my book *Christian Counselling and Occultism*, he decided to enter into the type of work I had described. After a year, in which he had counselled a number of people, he went out of his mind. Shortly after this he died.

An evangelist who accompanied me during some of my meetings in England felt called to a similar work among the occultly oppressed. However, it was more a matter of the right method for him than a case of spiritual authority. After two years he gave up this special type of work, the devil having caused a serious set back in his life.

I travelled for a while in America with an American evangelist. He was encouraged through my lectures to start counselling people suffering from oppressions. Two years later his mind became confused and he had to go into a clinic for nervous disorders.

We should not allow these examples to take our courage away. We should rather use them to remind ourselves that the question is not that of adopting the right method of approach, but rather of having the spiritual authority required for this work. And if a person does not know how to distinguish between the two he should steer clear of this type of work.

C. Before counselling begins it is essential to diagnose correctly between mental illness and occult oppression. A person who is mentally ill must be treated by a psychiatrist. Naturally if possible one should seek out a Christian psychiatrist rather than a nominal Christian. The occultly oppressed on the other hand should turn to a qualified Christian worker for help. Failure to make the correct diagnosis leads sometimes to disastrous results. And it is not only counsellors who make these mistakes, but qualified psychiatrists as well.

D. The oppressed person must destroy any fetishes, idols or occult literature he has in his possession (Acts 19:19). Many missionaries make the mistake of regarding the idols and religious objects used by pagans in their various rites, as souvenir pieces, and as such accept them into their homes. The result is often an oppression falling on the whole family and their own lives. Figures which have been used in pagan rites act as crystallization points for demonic powers. This does not apply obviously to carvings which are merely designed for decorative use, although on the island of Bali in Indonesia every carved object is immediately consecrated to the devil when it is made, and hence should be avoided.

E.   An occultly oppressed person must break off relationships with any of his friends who continues to practice occultism, or who is affected by it, even if the person is his best friend (2 Corinthians 6:14; 1 Corinthians 10:20).

An example from the mission field. A man who belonged to a group of devil worshippers became a Christian, and as a result was set free. He was also healed of a longstanding illness at the time of his conversion. One day this new-born Christian visited some of his old friends. They were just about to have one of their religious meetings. Although the Christian took no part in the ceremonies which proceeded, he nevertheless stayed in the room till the service was over. The result was that his old illness returned. He should never have allowed himself to join with these devil worshippers again. God allows no one to make light of his demands.

F.   The confession of sins is mentioned in James 5:16. The word 'occult' means 'hidden'. The opposite to this is therefore 'to reveal'. It is only after recognition and confession of one's sins that one is able to stand before God. The confession, however, must cover a person's whole life, although such a confession must never be forced. Similarly one must not make a law that every single detail must be confessed before forgiveness is obtained. No man knows more than 1% of all his sins and guilt before God, and so we must rely on him to clean us from unknown sins (Psalm 19:12).

G. After the confession of one's sins it is essential through faith to appropriate the forgiveness which God promises to us (1 John 1:9). Without faith it is impossible to please God (Hebrews 11:6, Mark 9:23). The only way we can hope to realize any of the promises of the Word of God is through faith.

H. Many people who are occultly oppressed, however, find it almost impossible to believe. This is indeed one of the effects of the sins of sorcery. For this reason I often pray what one can call a prayer of renunciation with the person concerned. In 2 Corinthians 4:2 we read the words, "We have renounced the hidden things of shame" (Nestle Greek Interlinear). Such prayers of renunciation were already practiced in the early Church. Before a person was baptized he was asked, "Do you renounce the devil and all his works?" In response the candidate was expected to answer, "Yes, I renounce the devil and all his works." He was then baptized. In Latin this was called 'abrenuntiatio diaboli'. It still exists today in the liturgy of both the Catholic and the Lutheran Churches. In the counselling of the occultly oppressed, renunciation plays an important role. Every sin of sorcery is in effect a contract with the devil. These contracts have therefore to be officially cancelled and annulled through a prayer of renunciation.

I. Following confession and renunciation we have the absolution, the confirmation that a person's sins are forgiven (Mark 2:5, John 20:23). The counsellor is not able to dispense this absolution on his own authority. He merely acts as the mouth-piece of God.

J. A prayer of renunciation is basically some-thing that the oppressed person does for himself. The counsellor on occasions, how-ever, may find that he has to loose the person himself. This promise is based on Matthew 18:18. But a merely liturgical or methodical use of this promise will meet with no success. Loosing a person is essen-tially a charismatic task. Before a coun-sellor can take this step he must ascertain what God's will is. The counsellor who looses a person too quickly can come under heavy attack from Satan.

K. In difficult cases of oppression one needs

to form a prayer group to help the person get free. This idea is based on Matthew 18:19. Unfortunately there are very few groups of Christians willing to accept this task. In counselling demonically oppressed people, however, without this united effort one can often hope for little success. Let me give you an example.

A doctor had been practicing sorcery for many years. He came to see me on four occasions before he finally broke with his occult past. The bondage he was suffering from was so strong that it was necessary to form a prayer group who were ready to pray for him. For four months the group continued to pray regularly and intensively for the doctor. It was only then that the battle was finally won.

L.   In a number of cases of possession, prayer and fasting is an essential part of the deliverance. As Jesus said in Matthew 17:21, "This kind never comes out except by prayer and fasting." Fasting is not a means of forcing God's hands, but merely a support for earnest prayer.

M.   Any counsellor who ventures into the field we have been talking about must place himself daily and hourly under the protection of the Lord. I know from my own experience that if the Lord had not stepped in to protect me, my work among the demonically oppressed would have ruined me long ago. It is a triumph of the grace of

God that I have been able to serve him all these years.

But it is not only the counsellor who needs to put himself under the daily protection of the blood of Jesus. The person who has been delivered must also learn to flee to the cross of Christ. We are too weak in ourselves to stand up to all the powers of darkness. It is only in Christ that we can stand. "His name has made this man strong!" (Acts 3:16).

N. The devil sometimes entangles the counsellor and attacks him severely. God, however, has placed an excellent weapon in our hands to deal with situations like this: the right to command the devil in the name of Jesus. The apostle Paul himself used this right at Philippi (Acts 16:18). The person seeking deliverance must also learn to command in the name of the Lord. He must not just remain passive, but must take hold of the sword of the Spirit himself and learn to use it (Ephesians 6:17).

I came across a good example of commanding in Christ's name in the spring of 1972. It was told to me by the Rev. Henry Dyck (First Mennonite Church, Kelowna BC).

In the autumn of 1971, the Lord sent a revival to the Ebenezer Baptist Church (Rev. W. L. McLeod) and the Alliance Church (Rev. W. Boldt) in Saskatoon, Canada. By early 1972 the flame had spread to Kelowna. The first church to experience the revival there was that of Rev. Babbel, but it soon spread to other churches as well. Many ministers who had been Christians for years were moved afresh by the Lord.

At the same time the power of the Lord Jesus was seen to be at work in the signs which followed. This brings me to the example which I mentioned above and which illustrates the right of a Christian to command in the name of Jesus. The eleven-year-old son of a minister came across a group of boys at the Wood Lake Elementary School who were playing with a ouija-board. The oiuja-board is a spiritistic piece of apparatus through which one can contact not only the subconscious mind but also the spirit world. It is particularly effective when someone is present who has mediumistic powers.

The pupils were playing with the board which was giving answers to all the question they put to it. Suddenly one of the boys asked, "Where do you get your power from?" The ouija-board answered, "From Hitler." The boy replied, "Come on, don't kid us, tell us the truth." This time the ouija-board replied, "Lucifer." The pupils did not understand what the word meant, so they asked "Who?" "Satan," was the reply.

The eleven-year-old minister's son who had also been affected by the revival, felt duty bound because of the faith to do something. Therefore, turning to the board he said, "In the name of the Lord Jesus I condemn you." From that moment on the ouija-board went dead, and gave no more answers at all.

One of the other boys who watched all this take place reacted by saying, "If that's the kind of power there is in the name of Jesus, then I'm going to start going to Sunday School to get to know more about him."

O.   Just as the body needs food, so our spiritual nature needs nourishment (Acts 2:42). The Christian who fails to make use of these 'means of grace' - God's Word, fellowship, communion, prayer - will not be able to stand in the fight.

P.   Anyone who finds himself involved in this battle, and that includes the counsellor as much as the oppressed person himself, must put on the whole armour of God (Ephesians 6:10-18). People have often asked me how we should make use of these weapons. What we have to do is to activate the Word of God in our lives by means of the promises of the Holy Spirit. Let me explain. In my own life I have often experienced times when I have felt downcast and almost in despair. At such times, however, the Holy Spirit has somehow brought certain passages of the Bible home to me with renewed force. Let me quote a few:

Joel 2:21 — Be glad and rejoice, the Lord has done great things.

Mark 6:50 — Jesus said to them, "Take heart, it is I; have no fear."

Isaish 66:2 — This is the man to whom I will look, he that is humble and contrite in spirit, and trembles at my Word.

Deut. 1:29, 30 — "Do not be in dread or afraid of them. The Lord your God who goes before you will himself fight for you."

Deut. 33:3 — All those consecrated to him were in his hands.

Psalm 73:28 — But for me it is good to be near God; I have made the Lord God my refuge, that I may tell of all thy works.

2 Tim. 4:17 — But the Lord stood by me and gave me strength.

Nehemiah 8:10 — Do not be grieved, for the joy of the Lord is your strength.

Isaiah 57:18 — I have seen his ways, but I will heal him; I will lead him and requite him with comfort.

Jer. 50:34 — Their redeemer is strong; the Lord of Hosts is his Name.

When the battle rages around us we will find that God's words are a strong fortress, they are a rock upon which we can safely build.

Q. The Lord expects us to reckon on the

victory he has won. When the children of
Israel began to despair before the Red Sea
(Exodus 14:13, 14) they realized suddenly
that God had already planned the victory.
When there seemed to be no hope left, God
divided the waters. We too must reckon on
the victory which has already been prepared for us. As Paul wrote in 1 Corinthians 15:57, "Thanks be to God who gives
us the victory through our Lord Jesus
Christ." In every battle with the enemy we
must realize that the victory is ours.

R. Finally, Jesus warned us of the fact that
evil spirits which have been driven out of a
person can return again (Luke 11:24). If a
person does not understand the method of
the enemy's attack he can soon fall victim
to his wiles. The counsellor must therefore
make the delivered person aware of the fact
that the evil spirits will always try to find a
new point of attack.

   We must underline once more that
these eighteen points cannot be used like a
set of rules for counselling the occultly
oppressed. Jesus can in his sovereignty
bypass any or all of the steps, and give
lasting deliverance at once. My aim has
simply been to describe the weapons which
the Scriptures put at our disposal. Our duty
is but to "return to our homes and to declare how much God has done for us"
(Luke 8:39). We cannot do better than to
end now with some of the triumphant

words of the last book in the Bible on our lips:

"Worthy are you, our Lord God to receive glory and honor and power."

"You were slain and by your blood you ransomed men for God."

"Worthy is the Lamb to receive power and wealth and wisdom and might and honor and glory and blessing."

(Revelation 4:11, 5:9, 12)

THE END